1979 U.S.

YEARBOOK

ISBN: 9781793102102

This book gives a fascinating and informative insight into life in the United States in 1979. It includes everything from the most popular music of the year to the cost of a buying a new house. Additionally, there are chapters covering people in high office, the best-selling films of the year and all the main news and events. Want to know who won the World Series or which U.S. personalities were born in 1979? All this and much more awaits you within.

INDEX

FIRST EDITION

1979

January

S	M	T	W	T	F	S
	1	2	3	4	5	6
7	8	9	10	11	12	13
14	15	16	17	18	19	20
21	22	23	24	25	26	27
28	29	30	31			

◐:5 ○:13 ◑:21 ●:28

February

S	M	T	W	T	F	S
				1	2	3
4	5	6	7	8	9	10
11	12	13	14	15	16	17
18	19	20	21	22	23	24
25	26	27	28			

◐:3 ○:11 ◑:19 ●:26

March

S	M	T	W	T	F	S
				1	2	3
4	5	6	7	8	9	10
11	12	13	14	15	16	17
18	19	20	21	22	23	24
25	26	27	28	29	30	31

◐:5 ○:13 ◑:21 ●:27

April

S	M	T	W	T	F	S
1	2	3	4	5	6	7
8	9	10	11	12	13	14
15	16	17	18	19	20	21
22	23	24	25	26	27	28
29	30					

◐:4 ○:12 ◑:19 ●:26

May

S	M	T	W	T	F	S
		1	2	3	4	5
6	7	8	9	10	11	12
13	14	15	16	17	18	19
20	21	22	23	24	25	26
27	28	29	30	31		

◐:4 ○:11 ◑:18 ●:25

June

S	M	T	W	T	F	S
					1	2
3	4	5	6	7	8	9
10	11	12	13	14	15	16
17	18	19	20	21	22	23
24	25	26	27	28	29	30

◐:2 ○:10 ◑:17 ●:24

July

S	M	T	W	T	F	S
1	2	3	4	5	6	7
8	9	10	11	12	13	14
15	16	17	18	19	20	21
22	23	24	25	26	27	28
29	30	31				

◐:2 ○:9 ◑:16 ●:23

August

S	M	T	W	T	F	S
			1	2	3	4
5	6	7	8	9	10	11
12	13	14	15	16	17	18
19	20	21	22	23	24	25
26	27	28	29	30	31	

◐:1 ○:7 ◑:14 ●:22 ◐:30

September

S	M	T	W	T	F	S
						1
2	3	4	5	6	7	8
9	10	11	12	13	14	15
16	17	18	19	20	21	22
23	24	25	26	27	28	29
30						

○:6 ◑:13 ●:21 ◐:29

October

S	M	T	W	T	F	S
	1	2	3	4	5	6
7	8	9	10	11	12	13
14	15	16	17	18	19	20
21	22	23	24	25	26	27
28	29	30	31			

○:5 ◑:12 ●:20 ◐:28

November

S	M	T	W	T	F	S
				1	2	3
4	5	6	7	8	9	10
11	12	13	14	15	16	17
18	19	20	21	22	23	24
25	26	27	28	29	30	

○:4 ◑:11 ●:19 ◐:26

December

S	M	T	W	T	F	S
						1
2	3	4	5	6	7	8
9	10	11	12	13	14	15
16	17	18	19	20	21	22
23	24	25	26	27	28	29
30	31					

○:3 ◑:11 ●:19 ◐:26

PEOPLE IN HIGH OFFICE

President: Jimmy Carter

January 20, 1977 - January 20, 1981 / Democratic Party

Born October 1, 1924 Jimmy Carter became the 39th President of the United States on January 20, 1977 after defeating incumbent President Gerald Ford. In 2012 Carter surpassed Herbert Hoover (31 years, 230 days) as the longest-retired president in U.S. history and is the first president to mark the 40th anniversary of his inauguration. Carter has remained active in public life during his post-presidency and in 2002 was awarded the Nobel Peace Prize for his work with the Carter Center.

95th & 96th United States Congress

Vice President	Walter Mondale
Chief Justice	Warren E. Burger
Speaker of the House	Tip O'Neill
Senate Majority Leader	Robert Byrd

U.S. Flag - 50 stars (1960-Present)

United Kingdom

Monarch
Queen Elizabeth II
February 6, 1952 -
Present

Prime Minister
James Callaghan
April 5, 1976 -
May 4, 1979

Prime Minister
Margaret Thatcher
May 4, 1979 -
November 28, 1990

Australia

Soviet Union

Ireland

Prime Minister
Malcom Fraser
November 11, 1975 -
March 11, 1983

Communist Party Leader
Leonid Brezhnev
October 14, 1964 -
November 10, 1982

Taoiseach
Jack Lynch
July 5, 1977 -
December 11, 1979

Brazil

President
Ernesto Geisel (1974-1979)
João Figueiredo (1979-1985)

Canada

Prime Minister
Pierre Trudeau (1968-1979)
Joe Clark (1979-1980)

China

Communist Party Leader
Hua Guofeng (1976-1981)

Cuba

President
Fidel Castro (1976-2008)

France

President
Valéry Giscard d'Estaing (1974-1981)

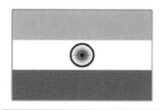

India

Prime Minister
Morarji Desai (1977-1979)
Charan Singh (1979-1980)

Israel

Prime Minister
Menachem Begin (1977-1983)

Italy

Prime Minister
Giulio Andreotti (1976-1979)
Francesco Cossiga (1979-1980)

Japan — Prime Minister Masayoshi Ōhira (1978-1980)

Mexico — President José López Portillo (1976-1982)

New Zealand — Prime Minister Robert Muldoon (1975-1984)

Pakistan — President Muhammad Zia-ul-Haq (1978-1988)

South Africa — Prime Minister P. W. Botha (1978-1984)

Spain — Prime Minister Adolfo Suárez (1976-1981)

Turkey — Prime Minister Bülent Ecevit (1978-1979) Süleyman Demirel (1979-1980)

West Germany — Chancellor Helmut Schmidt (1974-1982)

U.S. NEWS & EVENTS

JAN

	January 1 to 31: Averaged over the contiguous United States this is the coldest month since modern global record-keeping started in 1880. The mean temperature for the month was 21.90°F (-5.61°C).
1	The United States and the People's Republic of China establish full diplomatic relations.
4	The State of Ohio agrees to pay $675,000 to families of those who were killed or injured in the Kent State shootings of May 4, 1970. *History: The Kent State shootings occurred when members of the Ohio National Guard opened fire on unarmed college students at Kent State University during a mass protest against the bombing of Cambodia by U.S. military forces. Twenty-eight guardsmen fired approximately 67 rounds over a period of 13 seconds killing four students and wounding nine others, one of whom suffered permanent paralysis.*
9	The Music for UNICEF Concert is held at the United Nations General Assembly in New York City to raise money for UNICEF and promote the Year of the Child. Hosted by The Bee Gees, other performers include Donna Summer, John Denver, Olivia Newton-John, ABBA, Rod Stewart and Earth, Wind & Fire.
9	Hockey legend Bobby Orr's #4 jersey is retired by the Boston Bruins.
12	The 6th American Music Awards are held; Barry Manilow, Linda Ronstadt and the Bee Gees are amongst the winners.

January 13: Chicago blizzard: A major blizzard strikes northern Illinois and northwest Indiana. It lasts for a total of 38 hours and is one of the largest Chicago snowstorms in history (at the time) with 21 inches of snowfall. Five people die during the blizzard and approximately 15 others are seriously injured due to conditions created by the storm. One of the five deaths came when a snowplow driver went berserk, hitting 34 cars and then backing into a rolled over a car behind him, killing the passenger.

19	Former Attorney General John N. Mitchell is released on parole after serving 19 months at a federal prison in Alabama due to the multiple crimes he committed in the Watergate affair.

January 21: Super Bowl XIII: The Pittsburgh Steelers defeat the Dallas Cowboys 35-31 at the Miami Orange Bowl in Miami, Florida in front of 79,484 fans. The MVP is #12 Terry Bradshaw, the Steelers quarterback.

23	Willie Mays, nicknamed 'The Say Hey Kid', is elected to the Baseball Hall of Fame.
26	'The Dukes of Hazzard' premieres on CBS. *Fun Fact: The series was inspired by the 1975 film Moonrunners, and ran for 7 seasons (147 episodes).*
27	The 36th Golden Globe Awards take place honoring the best in film and television for 1978. The winners include Midnight Express, Jon Voight and Jane Fonda.
29	Brenda Ann Spencer opens fire at the Grover Cleveland Elementary School in San Diego, California, killing two faculty members and wounding eight students. Her response to the action, "I don't like Mondays," inspired the Boomtown Rats to make a song of the same name.

FEB

4	The 29th NBA All-Star Game is played at the Pontiac Silverdome in the Detroit suburb of Pontiac, Michigan. The West beats East 134-129 in front of 31,745 spectators.
11	43 million people watch the made-for-television biographical film 'Elvis' on ABC. The film was directed by John Carpenter and starred Kurt Russell as Elvis Presley.
13	An intense windstorm strikes western Washington and sinks a ½-mile-long section of the Hood Canal Bridge (officially William A. Bugge Bridge). At the time of the failure the bridge had been closed to highway traffic and the tower crew had evacuated; there were no casualties. *Fun Fact: First opened in 1961 it is the longest floating bridge in the world located in a saltwater tidal basin, and the third longest floating bridge overall.*

14	In Kabul, Muslim extremists kidnap the American ambassador to Afghanistan, Adolph Dubs. Dubs is later killed during a gunfight between his kidnappers and police.
15	The 21st Grammy Awards, recognizing accomplishments by musicians from the year 1978, is held at the Shrine Auditorium, Los Angeles, California. The record / song of the year is Billy Joel's 'Just the Way You Are' and the best new artist is A Taste of Honey.
24	The highest price ever paid for a pig is negotiated by breeder Russ Baize in Stamford, Texas. Baize paid $42,500 for a boar named 'Glacier' - the record stands for eighteen years.
26	A total solar eclipse occurs in North America. *Fun Fact: It would be 38 years, August 21, 2017, before the next total solar eclipse would be visible across North America (the next one will be April 8, 2024).*
27	The annual Mardi Gras celebration in New Orleans, Louisiana is canceled due to a strike called by the New Orleans Police Department.

MAR

4	U.S. Voyager I space probe photos reveal the first evidence of a ring around the planet Jupiter.
7	Warren Giles and Hack Wilson are elected to baseball Hall of Fame.
7	The 5th People's Choice Awards honoring the best in popular culture for 1978 is broadcast on CBS. The winners include Burt Reynolds, Olivia Newton-John, Billy Joel, Andy Gibb, Alan Alda, Robin Williams, Mary Tyler Moore and Carol Burnett.
23	Larry Holmes TKOs Osvaldo Ocasio in 7 rounds at the Hilton, Winchester, Nevada to retain the WBC heavyweight boxing title.

March 25: The first fully functional space shuttle orbiter, Columbia, is delivered to the John F. Kennedy Space Center, to be prepared for its first launch. *Columbia was originally scheduled to lift off in late 1979, however the launch date was delayed by problems with both the Space Shuttle main engine and the thermal protection system. It eventually made the first flight of the Space Shuttle program on April 12, 1982. Over 22 years of service it completed 27 missions before disintegrating during re-entry near the end of its 28th mission on February 1, 2003 - the tragedy resulted in the deaths of all seven crew members.*

March 26: In a ceremony at the White House President Jimmy Carter witnesses President Anwar Sadat of Egypt and Prime Minister Menachem Begin of Israel sign the Egyptian-Israeli Peace Treaty.

27	The Supreme Court rules in an 8-1 decision that the Fourth Amendment bars the police from stopping motorists at random merely to check licenses and auto registrations.
29	America's most serious nuclear power plant accident occurs in reactor No.2 of the Three Mile Island Nuclear Generating Station in Dauphin County, Pennsylvania. The partial meltdown resulted in the release of radioactive gases and radioactive iodine into the environment and was rated a five on the seven-point International Nuclear Event Scale. *Follow Up: The cleanup started in August 1979 and officially ended in December 1993 - the total cost of the cleanup was around $1 billion.*

APR

9	The 51st Academy Awards honoring films released in 1978 takes place at the Dorothy Chandler Pavilion in Los Angeles. The Deer Hunter wins five awards including Best Picture, and Jon Voight and Jane Fonda win the best actor / actress awards.
10	A tornado hits Wichita Falls, Texas, killing 42 and causing $400 million in damage.
16	The Pulitzer Prize is awarded to Sam Shepard for his play 'Buried Child'.
18	The reality television series 'Real People' premieres on NBC. The show features 'real people' (as opposed to celebrities) with unique occupations or hobbies and runs for 5 seasons.

APR

20	President Jimmy Carter is attacked by a swamp rabbit while fishing in his hometown of Plains, Georgia.
22	The Albert Einstein Memorial is unveiled at The National Academy of Sciences in Washington, DC in honor of the centennial of Einstein's birth. *History: Albert Einstein (b. March 14, 1879 - d. April 18, 1955) was a German-born theoretical physicist who developed the theory of relativity, one of the two pillars of modern physics (alongside quantum mechanics). His work is also known for its influence on the philosophy of science. He is though best known to the general public for his mass-energy equivalence formula $E = mc^2$, which has been dubbed "the world's most famous equation".*

MAY

	The unemployment rate drops to 5.6%, the low point for the late 1970s business cycle and the lowest since July 1974.
2	The 14th Academy of Country Music Awards are held at The Palladium, Los Angeles, California honoring the best of country music from 1978. The winners include Kenny Rogers, Barbara Mandrell, Randy Goodrum's "You Needed Me" and "Tulsa Time" by Don Williams.
9	Northwestern University graduate student John Harris suffers minor cuts and burns after a detonator goes off inside a cigar case left by the Unabomber Ted Kaczynski - the actual bomb fails to explode.
12	Chris Evert's 125-match clay court winning streak comes to an end - she was finally beaten in a third-set tiebreak, 6-4, 2-6, 7-6, in the semi-finals of the Italian Open against Tracy Austin. The streak ran from August 1973 and encompassed 24 tournaments. *Fun Fact: Evert became the first player, male or female, to win 1,000 professional singles matches.*
21	In San Francisco, gay people riot after hearing the verdict for Dan White, assassin of Mayor George Moscone and Supervisor Harvey Milk on Monday, November 27, 1978 - After thirty-six hours of deliberation the jury had found White guilty of voluntary manslaughter rather than first-degree murder.
21	The Montréal Canadiens defeat the New York Rangers 4 games to 1 for their fourth consecutive Stanley Cup championship.
25	American Airlines Flight 191: In Chicago a DC-10 crashes during take-off at O'Hare International Airport killing 258 passengers, 13 crew and 2 people on the ground. With 273 fatalities it was the deadliest aviation accident to have occurred in the United States to that date.
25	Convicted murderer John Spenkelink is executed in Florida in the first use of the electric chair in America since the reintroduction of death penalty in 1976.
25	Six-year-old Etan Kalil Patz disappears on his way to his school bus stop in the SoHo neighborhood of Lower Manhattan, New York City. *Follow Up: Etan becomes one of the first children to be profiled on the "photo on a milk carton" campaigns of the early 1980s, and in 1983, President Ronald Reagan designates May 25 - the anniversary of his disappearance - as National Missing Children's Day in the U.S. It is later determined that Etan had been abducted and murdered the same day that he went missing by Pedro Hernandez. Hernandez was found guilty and sentenced to 25-years-to-life in prison on April 18, 2017.*

MAY

25	The movie 'Alien', directed by Ridley Scott and starring Sigourney Weaver, is released in the U.S. *The success of Alien spawned a media franchise of films, novels, comic books, video games, and toys. It also launched Weaver's acting career, providing her with her first lead role.*
27	Rick Mears wins the Indianapolis 500 for the first time (his other wins in the race come in 1984, 1988 and 1991).

JUN

	McDonald's introduces the first national Happy Meal - it has a circus wagon train theme and costs $1.00.
1	The Seattle SuperSonics take the NBA Championship, 4 games to 1, against the Washington Bullets.
3	The 33rd Annual Tony Awards are broadcast by CBS television from the Shubert Theatre in New York City. The best play award goes to "The Elephant Man" and best musical to "Sweeny Todd". Tom Conti, Constance Cummings and Carole Shelley win the awards for best leading actor / actresses in a play.
13	The U.S. Court of Claims, with 5-2 majority, decides that the 1877 Act that seized the Black Hills from the Sioux was a violation of the Fifth Amendment.
18	Jimmy Carter and Leonid Brezhnev sign the SALT II (Strategic Arms Limitation Talks) agreement in Vienna.
20	A Nicaraguan National Guard soldier kills ABC TV news correspondent Bill Stewart and his interpreter Juan Espinosa. Other members of the news crew capture the killing on tape.
22	Larry Holmes TKOs Mike Weaver in 12 rounds at Madison Square Garden, New York City to retain the WBC heavyweight boxing title.

JUL

2	The Susan B. Anthony dollar is introduced in the U.S. *Fun Fact: 500 million coins had been stockpiled prior to release because mint officials feared that the coins would be hoarded upon release.*
3	President Carter signs the first directive for secret aid to the opponents of the pro-Soviet regime in Kabul.
10	Chuck Berry is sentenced to four months in prison for income tax evasion with $200,000 worth of unpaid taxes. He is also required to complete 1,000 hours of community service, which he fulfils by doing benefit concerts.
11	NASA's first orbiting space station Skylab starts to disintegrate as it re-enters the atmosphere after being in orbit for 6 years and 2 months.
12	A Disco Demolition Night publicity stunt goes awry at Comiskey Park, Illinois, forcing the Chicago White Sox to forfeit the second game of a double-header against the Detroit Tigers. 50,000 spectators had turned up (35,000 more than usual) to watch the game and a crate filled with disco records being blown up on the field. The playing field was so damaged by the explosion, and by fans rushing on to it, that the White Sox were required to forfeit the game.
17	Nicaraguan dictator General Anastasio Somoza DeBayle resigns and flees to Miami, Florida - Somoza is denied entry to the U.S. by President Carter and later takes refuge in Paraguay.

5	Willie Mays, Warren Giles, and Hack Wilson are inducted into the Baseball Hall of Fame in Cooperstown, Central New York.
6	A 5.7Mw earthquake occurs on the Calaveras Fault near Coyote Lake in Santa Clara County, California. It has a maximum Mercalli intensity of VII (very strong) and causes 16 injuries, and $500,000 in damage.
9	Raymond Washington, co-founder of the Crips (today one of the largest, most notorious gangs in the U.S.), is murdered in a drive-by shooting. His killers have never been identified.

August 10: Michael Jackson releases his first breakthrough album 'Off the Wall' - the album goes on to sell over 8 million copies in the United States alone. *Fun Facts: Michael Jackson is one of the few artists to have been inducted into the Rock and Roll Hall of Fame twice. He has also been inducted into the Songwriters Hall of Fame and the Dance Hall of Fame as the only dancer from pop and rock music. His other achievements include multiple Guinness World Records including the Most Successful Entertainer of All Time, 13 Grammy Awards, the Grammy Legend Award, the Grammy Lifetime Achievement Award, 24 American Music Awards - more than any other artist - including the "Artist of the Century", 13 number-one singles in the U.S. during his solo career - more than any other male artist in the Hot 100 era - and estimated sales of over 350 million records worldwide. His follow up album to Off the Wall, Thriller, is the best-selling album of all time, with estimated sales of over 66 million copies worldwide.*

15	'Apocalypse Now', directed by Francis Ford Coppola and starring Marlon Brando, Robert Duvall, and Martin Sheen, is released.

SEP

1	The 571lb robotic space probe Pioneer 11 becomes the first spacecraft to visit Saturn - at its closest point it passes the planet at a distance of 13,000 miles.
3	Jerry Lewis' 14th Muscular Dystrophy telethon raises $30,075,227, up 5.56% on the previous year.

9	The 31st Emmy Awards, hosted by Henry Winkler from the Pasadena Civic Auditorium, are broadcast on ABC. The winners include the sitcom Taxi, drama series Lou Grant, actors Carroll O'Connor and Ron Leibman, and actresses Ruth Gordon and Mariette Hartley.
12	Hurricane Frederic makes landfall at 10:00pm on Alabama's Gulf Coast. Five people are killed by Frederic but the damage accrued, $1.77 billion (equivalent to $6.15 billion in 2018), makes it the Atlantic basin's costliest tropical cyclone on record at the time.
23	The largest anti-nuclear demonstration to date is held in New York City, with almost 200,000 people in attendance. *The New York rally was held in conjunction with a series of nightly 'No Nukes' concerts given at Madison Square Garden (September 19 through 23).*
26	In one of the most expensive transactions in the history of television, ABC wins the television rights to the 1984 Summer Olympic Games in Los Angeles with a bid of $225 million.
28	Larry Holmes TKOs Earnie Shavers in 11 rounds at Caesars Palace, Paradise, Nevada, to retain the WBC heavyweight boxing title.

OCT

Pope John Paul II greets 80,000 people at the old Yankee Stadium, New York City.

October 1-8: Pope John Paul II makes his first pastoral visit the United States stopping over in Boston, New York City, Philadelphia, Des Moines, Chicago and Washington, D.C. *Fun Facts: Born in Poland in 1920, John Paul II was the second longest-serving Pope (1978-2005) in modern history after Pope Pius IX. During his reign the 'Pilgrim Pope', he made 104 foreign trips (7 to the U.S.) and visited 129 countries, more than all previous Popes combined and logging more than 725,000 miles (1,167,000km). He was declared a saint on April 27, 2014 by Pope Francis.*

OCT

8	The 13th Country Music Association Awards take place recognizing outstanding achievements in the country music industry. Winners include Willie Nelson, Kenny Rogers and Barbara Mandrell.
12	Future Basketball Hall of Fame forward Earvin 'Magic' Johnson makes his debut for Los Angeles Lakers against the San Diego Clippers; the Lakers win 103-102.
14	The 'National March on Washington for Lesbian and Gay Rights' takes place in Washington, D.C. The rally draws between 75,000 and 125,000 participants demanding equal civil rights, and urging the passage of protective civil rights legislation.
15	A 6.5Mw earthquake affects Imperial Valley in Southern California, and Mexicali Valley in northern Baja California. It has a maximum Mercalli intensity of IX (violent) and causes 91 injuries, and $30 million in damage. *At the time it is the largest earthquake to occur in the contiguous United States since the 1971 San Fernando earthquake eight years earlier.*
17	President Carter signs a law establishing the Department of Education; the department becomes operational on May 4, 1980.
17	The Pittsburgh Pirates defeat the Baltimore Orioles by 4 games to 3 to take the 1979 World Series.
22	Mickey Mouse welcomes Walt Disney World Magic Kingdom's 100-millionth visitor, 8-year-old Kurt Miller from Kingsville, Maryland. He receives a lifetime pass from Mickey and WDW Vice President Bob Allen. *Fun Fact: Walt Disney World's Magic Kingdom has the highest annual attendance of any amusement park in the world; it had 20,450,000 visitors in 2017.*

NOV

2	Assata Shakur (born Joanne Byron), a former member of Black Panther Party and Black Liberation Army, escapes from Clinton Correctional Facility for Women in New Jersey. *Follow Up: Shakur eventually surfaced in Cuba in 1984 where she was granted political asylum. She still resides in Cuba today.*
3	The Greensboro massacre takes place during a "Death to the Klan" march in Greensboro, North Carolina. Members of the Communist Workers' Party and others, advocating that Klan members should be "physically beaten and chased out of town", engaged in a shootout with members of the Ku Klux Klan and the American Nazi Party. Four members of the CWP and one other individual were killed, and eleven other demonstrators and a Klansman were wounded.
4	Iran hostage crisis begins: 500 Iranian students loyal to Ayatollah Khomeini seize the U.S. Embassy in Tehran. They take 90 hostages (53 of whom are American) and demand that the United States return the former Shah of Iran to stand trial and execution.
9	NORAD computers at the Alternate National Military Command Center in Fort Ritchie, Maryland, detect a purported massive Soviet nuclear strike. Strategic Air Command are notified and nuclear bombers prepared for takeoff. Within six to seven minutes of the initial response satellite and radar systems are able to confirm that the attack is a false alarm - it was found that a training scenario had been inadvertently loaded into an operational computer.

14	Iran hostage crisis: President Carter issues Executive Order 12170, the freezing all Iranian assets in the U.S.
15	A package from the Unabomber Ted Kaczynski begins smoking in the cargo hold of American Airlines Flight 444 from Chicago to Washington, D.C., forcing the plane to make an emergency landing. The twelve passengers suffer non-lethal smoke inhalation. *Follow Up: Between 1978 and 1995 the Unabomber killed three people and injured 23 others. After his arrest in 1996 Kaczynski tried unsuccessfully to dismiss his court-appointed lawyers because they wanted him to plead insanity in order to avoid the death penalty, and he did not believe he was insane. In 1998 a plea bargain was reached under which he pleaded guilty to all charges and was sentenced to life in prison without the possibility of parole.*
17	Iranian leader Ruhollah Khomeini orders the release of 13 female and African American hostages being held at the U.S. Embassy in Tehran.
25	Pat Summerall and John Madden are paired together for the first time, a pairing that would last 22 years and become one of the most well-known partnerships in TV sportscasting history.

DEC

3	Eleven fans are killed during a stampede for seats before the British rock band the Who perform at Riverfront Coliseum in Cincinnati, Ohio - the concert went on as planned, with the band members not told of the tragedy until after their performance.
6	The world premiere of Star Trek: The Motion Picture, directed by Robert Wise, starring William Shatner and Leonard Nimoy, is held at the Smithsonian Institution in Washington, D.C.

December 17: The three wheeled Budweiser Rocket car driven by Stanley Barrett claims to break the sound barrier by reaching a speed of 739.666mph, or Mach 1.01, during a run on Rogers Dry Lake at Edwards AFB (although no independent authority has sanctioned the performance). *Fun Fact: The British Thrust SSC became the first officially recognized car to break the sound barrier in 1997 with an average speed of 763.035mph (1227.99km/h) on a measured mile in both directions. The Trust SSC weighed nearly 10 tons and had a total thrust of 223kN.*

30 WORLDWIDE NEWS & EVENTS

1. January 25: Pope John Paul II visits the Dominican Republic on his first overseas trip as supreme pontiff.
2. February 1: Ayatollah Khomeini returns in triumph to Iran after 14 years in exile and is welcomed by a joyous crowd estimated to be around five million people.
3. February 7: Pluto enters a 20-year period inside the orbit of Neptune for the first time in 230 years.
4. February 20: In Northern Ireland eleven loyalists known as the "Shankill Butchers" are sentenced to life in prison for 19 murders.
5. March 1: Philips publicly demonstrates a prototype of an optical digital audio disc at a press conference in Eindhoven, Netherlands.
6. March 31: The 24th Eurovision Song Contest is held at the International Convention Center in Jerusalem, Israel and the 19 countries taking part see Israel win for the second year running. The winning song "Hallelujah" was performed by Gali Atari and Milk and Honey.
7. April 2: The world's first anthrax epidemic begins in Ekaterinburg, Russia following a biological weapons plant accident. The ensuing outbreak of the disease results in approximately 100 deaths.
8. April 13: The longest ever doubles ping-pong match ends after 101 hours, 11 minutes and 11 seconds. The match was contested by brothers Lance, Phil and Mark Warren, and their friend Bill Weir at Sacramento, California.
9. April 17: Four Royal Ulster Constabulary officers are killed by a Provisional Irish Republican Army bomb in Bessbrook, County Armagh; the roadside van bomb is believed to be the largest used by the IRA up to that point.
10. May 4: Margaret Thatcher becomes the first woman to be elected Prime Minister of the United Kingdom as the Conservatives win the British General Election with a 43-seat majority.

11. May 21: Elton John becomes the first megastar to perform live in the Soviet Union. The tour consists of eight concerts in total: four at the Great October Hall in Leningrad (now Saint Petersburg), and four more at the Rossya Hotel in Moscow. He also plays a spontaneous set at a Moscow restaurant.

12. May 24: The 32nd Cannes Film Festival comes to a close. Apocalypse Now, directed by Francis Ford Coppola, and Die Biechtrommel, directed by Volker Schlondorff, are jointly awarded the Palme d'Or.

13. June 4: Joe Clark is sworn in as the youngest Prime Minister in Canadian history, taking office the day before his 40th birthday. In so doing he defeats the Liberal government of Pierre Trudeau and ends sixteen years of continuous Liberal rule.

14. June 12: Bryan Allen, flying the Gossamer Albatross, becomes the first person to cross the English Channel in a human-powered aircraft. He completed the crossing in 2 hours and 49 minutes to win the £100,000 Kremer Prize. The aircraft was designed and built by a team led by Dr. Paul B. MacCready, a noted American aeronautics engineer, designer, and world soaring champion.

15. July 1: Sony introduces the Walkman TPS-L2, a blue and silver cassette player that runs off two AA batteries. Initially released in Japan, the company predicted only 5,000 would sell but instead its popularity skyrocketed and within the first two months Sony sold more than 50,000 Walkmans costing around $200 each. *Fun Facts: The original idea for a portable stereo is credited to Brazilian-German inventor Andreas Pavel who patented the Stereobelt in 1977. Though Sony agreed to pay Pavel royalties, it refused to recognize him as the inventor of the personal stereo until a legal settlement in 2003. The Walkman sold in excess of 385 million units between 1979 and 2009.*

16. July 5: Queen Elizabeth II presides over the 1000th annual open-air sitting of the Isle of Man's Parliament at Tynwald.

17. July 16: President Hasan al-Bakr resigns and is succeeded by Vice President Saddam Hussein in Iraq.

18. July 19: Two gigantic supertankers, the Atlantic Empress and the Aegean Captain, collide off the island of Tobago in the Caribbean Sea, killing 26 crew members and spilling 280,000 tons of crude oil into the sea.

19. July 22: The 66th Tour de France come to a close after 24 stages covering a total distance of 2,339 miles (3,765km). For the second year running the winner was Bernard Hinault of France. *Fun Fact: Hinault won the race a total of five times - 1978, 1979, 1981, 1982 and 1985.*

20. August 17: Monty Python's 'Life of Brian', directed by Terry Jones, premieres in the U.S. The film tells the story of Brian Cohen (played by Graham Chapman), a young Jewish man who is born on the same day as, and next door to, Jesus Christ, and is subsequently mistaken for the Messiah.

21. August 21: Daniel E. Chadwick is granted a patent for his invention, the snowboard.

22.	August 27: Lord Mountbatten of Burma, his nephew Nicholas, and a boatboy Paul Maxwell, are assassinated by a Provisional Irish Republican Army bomb while holidaying in the Republic of Ireland. The Dowager Lady Brabourne also dies from her injuries the following day in hospital.
23.	October 11: Godfrey Hounsfield wins the Nobel Prize in Physiology or Medicine jointly with Allan McLeod Cormack for his part in developing the diagnostic technique of X-ray computed tomography (the CT scan).
24.	October 27: Mother Teresa of Calcutta (b. Anjezë Gonxhe Bojaxhiu, August 26, 1910 - d. September 5, 1997) is awarded Nobel Peace Prize. *Fun Fact: Mother Teresa was declared a saint by Pope Francis in 2016.*
25.	December: The World Health Organization certifies the global eradication of smallpox. *Historic Facts: The earliest evidence of smallpox dates back to the 3rd century BC in Egyptian mummies. In the 20th century it is estimated that smallpox resulted in 300-500 million deaths - the last naturally occurring case was diagnosed in October 1977.*
26.	December 1: The world's first mobile phone network, NTT is launched into commercial operation in Tokyo, Japan.
27.	December 3: Ayatollah Ruhollah Khomeini becomes the first Supreme Leader of Iran.

28. December 10: 20-year-old daredevil Eddie Kidd performs a 100mph "death-defying" 80ft jump, over a 50ft sheer drop, on his 400cc motorcycle. Kidd completed the stunt before a stunned group of spectators, fans and press, over the River Blackwater in Essex, England. *Career Highlights: Eddie Kidd won the stunt bike world championship in 1993 over Robbie Knievel, son of Evel Knievel. He also jumped the Great Wall of China in 1993 and had parts in several movies before being paralysed in an accident in 1996. He became received an OBE in 2012 for his services to charity.*

29.	December 15: Whilst playing Scrabble and drinking beer Canadians Chris Haney and Scott Abbott decide to create their own game - Trivial Pursuit. *Fun Facts: The game was released in 1981 and since then has sold more 100 million copies in 26 countries. Total estimated sales are around $2 billion.*
30.	December 24: The Ariane 1 rocket makes its maiden flight. Developed and operated by the European Space Agency, it was the first launcher developed with the primary purpose of sending commercial satellites into geosynchronous orbit.

BIRTHS
U.S. PERSONALITIES
BORN IN 1979

Drew Christopher Brees
January 15, 1979

Football quarterback for the New Orleans Saints of the NFL. Brees holds the NFL records for career pass completions, completion percentage and passing yards, and in 2012 broke Johnny Unitas' long-standing record of consecutive games with a touchdown pass. He has passed for over 5,000 yards in a season five times and has led the NFL in passing yards a record seven times. Brees was the MVP of Super Bowl XLIV and Sports Illustrated named him its 2010 Sportsman of the Year.

Aaliyah Dana Haughton
January 16, 1979 -
August 25, 2001

Singer, actress, and model. Aaliyah first gained recognition at the age of 10 when she appeared on the television show Star Search and performed in concert alongside Gladys Knight. Her uncle Barry Hankerson introduced her to R. Kelly, who became her mentor, as well as lead songwriter and producer of her debut album, Age Ain't Nothing but a Number. Aaliyah has been credited for helping redefine contemporary R&B, pop and hip hop, and is estimated to have sold 32 million albums worldwide.

Brandy Rayana Norwood
February 11, 1979

Singer, songwriter, record producer, and actress known professionally by the mononym Brandy. Norwood signed with Atlantic Records in 1993 and the following year released her self-titled debut album which sold 6 million copies worldwide. In total she has sold over 30 million records to date and her work has earned her numerous awards and accolades including; a Grammy Award, an American Music Award and seven Billboard Music Awards.

Jennifer Love Hewitt
February 21, 1979

Actress, singer, songwriter, producer and director. Hewitt received her breakthrough role as Sarah Reeves Merrin on the Fox teen drama Party of Five (1995-1999), and rose to fame as a teen star for her role as Julie James in the horror film I Know What You Did Last Summer (1997) and its 1998 sequel. More recent roles have included playing Melinda Gordon in Ghost Whisperer (2005-2010) and Special Agent Kate Callahan in Criminal Minds (2014-2015).

Adam Noah Levine
March 18, 1979

Lead singer for the pop rock band Maroon 5. In 2002 the band released their first album, 'Songs About Jane' which went multi-platinum. Since then they have released five more albums selling more than 70 million singles and 20 million albums worldwide. As part of Maroon 5 Levine has received three Grammy Awards, three American Music Awards, four Billboard Music Awards, an MTV Video Music Award and a World Music Award.

Norah Jones
March 30, 1979

Singer, songwriter, and pianist who was born Geethali Norah Jones Shankar. In 2002 she launched her solo music career when she released her debut album Come Away With Me. The record was certified Diamond and sold over 27 million copies. In total Jones has won 25 major awards throughout her career, including nine Grammys, and has sold more than 50 million records worldwide. In 2009 Billboard named her the top jazz artist of the decade 2000-2009.

Natasha Lyonne
April 4, 1979

Actress who is best known for her role as Nicky Nichols on the Netflix series Orange Is The New Black (2013-present), for which she received an Emmy Award nomination in 2014, and for her role as Jessica in the American Pie film series (1999-2012). During her career she has appeared in over 50 films, including: Everyone Says I Love You (1996), Scary Movie 2 (2001), Blade: Trinity (2004), Robots (2005), All About Evil (2010), Sleeping With Other People (2015), and Show Dogs (2017).

Claire Catherine Danes
April 12, 1979

Actress who gained early recognition as Angela Chase in the acclaimed 1994 teen drama series 'My So-Called Life'. She has had a number of both television and film roles since but is probably best known more recently for her lead role as Carrie Mathison in the Showtime drama series Homeland. Danes is the recipient of three Emmy Awards, four Golden Globe Awards and two Screen Actors Guild Awards. She was awarded a star on the Hollywood Walk of Fame in 2015.

Jennifer Marie Morrison
April 12, 1979

Actress, producer, director and former child model. As an actress she is best known for her roles as Dr. Allison Cameron in the medical-drama series House (2004-2012) and Emma Swan in the ABC adventure-fantasy series Once Upon a Time (2011-2018). She has also portrayed Zoey Pierson on the comedy series How I Met Your Mother, and Winona Kirk, mother of James T. Kirk, in the 2009 science-fiction film Star Trek. Morrison made her feature film directorial debut with Sun Dogs (2017).

Kourtney Mary Kardashian
April 18, 1979

Television personality, socialite, model and businesswoman. In 2007 she and her family were picked to star in the reality television series Keeping Up With The Kardashians. Its success led to the creation of spin-offs including Kourtney and Khloé Take Miami and Kourtney and Kim Take New York. Together with sisters Kim and Khloé, Kourtney has launched several clothing collections and fragrances, and additionally in 2010 released the book Kardashian Konfidential.

James Lance Bass
May 4, 1979

Singer, dancer, actor, film and television producer, and author. Bass rose to fame as a singer with the pop boy band NSYNC. As part of NSYNC, alongside Justin Timberlake, JC Chasez, Chris Kirkpatrick and Joey Fatone, the band sold over 70 million records and became the fifth-best-selling boy band in history. NSYNC's success led Bass to work in film and television and he starred in the 2001 film On the Line which his company Bacon & Eggs produced.

Christopher Michael Pratt
June 21, 1979

Actor who had his breakthrough role on television playing the character Bright Abbott on the WB drama Everwood (2002-2006), and then went on to earn further recognition for his role as Andy Dwyer on the NBC comedy series Parks And Recreation. Pratt achieved leading man status in 2014 starring in The Lego Movie and Guardians Of The Galaxy, and has continued this with leading roles in movies such as The Magnificent Seven (2016), and Avengers: Infinity War (2018).

Ryan Benjamin Tedder
June 26, 1979

Singer, songwriter, multi-instrumentalist, and record producer. As well as being the lead vocalist of the pop rock band OneRepublic, Tedder's production and songwriting work has proven commercially successful. Apologize, performed by his band OneRepublic, Bleeding Love, by Leona Lewis, and Halo, by Beyoncé, have all made it to the list of best-selling singles of all time. In early 2014 Billboard named him 'The Undercover King of Pop' and featured him on the magazine's cover.

Kevin Darnell Hart
July 6, 1979

Comedian, actor and television host who began his career by winning several amateur comedy competitions at clubs throughout New England, culminating in his first real break in 2001 when he was cast by Judd Apatow for a recurring role on the TV series Undeclared. Hart has starred in a number of films including Paper Soldiers (2002), Scary Movie 3 (2003), Soul Plane (2004), In the Mix (2005), Little Fockers (2010), Ride Along (2014) and The Secret Life Of Pets (2016).

Kimberly Susan Rhode
July 16, 1979

Double trap and skeet shooter who became the first Olympian to win an individual medal at six consecutive summer games when she won a bronze medal in Rio (2016). She is the most successful female shooter at the Olympics as the only triple Olympic Champion, and is only woman to have won two Olympic gold medals for Double Trap. She notably won her third gold medal in skeet shooting at the 2012 Summer Olympics, by equaling the world record of 99 out of 100 clays.

Joseph Jason Namakaeha Momoa
August 1, 1979

Actor, writer, director, producer and model who is known for his television roles as Ronon Dex on the military science fiction television series Stargate Atlantis (2004-2009), Khal Drogo in the HBO fantasy television series Game of Thrones (2011-2012), and as Declan Harp in the Netflix series Frontier (2016-present). In film Momoa has portrayed the title character in the sword and sorcery film Conan The Barbarian (2011), and plays Aquaman in the DC Extended Universe.

Aaron Paul Sturtevant
August 27, 1979

Actor primarily known for portraying Jesse Pinkman in the AMC series Breaking Bad (2008-2013) for which he won several awards for best supporting actor, including Primetime Emmy Awards in 2010, 2012 and 2014, and Saturn Awards in 2009, 2011 and 2013 (more than any other actor in that category). Since 2014 he has been the voice of Todd Chavez on the Netflix animated series BoJack Horseman, and has portrayed Eddie Lane in the Hulu drama series The Path (2016-2018).

Ruth Ellen Riley
August 28, 1979

Retired professional basketball player who played most recently for Atlanta Dream in the WNBA. Her Notre Dame team won the NCAA women's championship in 2001, and her Detroit Shock team won the WNBA championship in 2003 and 2006. Riley was the MVP in the 2001 and 2003 championship series, and became the first person to win the MVP awards in both the NCAA and the WNBA championships. She also played on the gold medal winning team at 2004 Athens Olympic Games.

Alecia Beth Moore
September 8, 1979

Singer, songwriter, dancer, and actress known professionally as Pink (stylized as P!nk). Originally a member of the girl group Choice in 1995, LaFace Records offered her a solo recording contract and her debut studio album, Can't Take Me Home (2000), was certified double-platinum. Since then Pink has sold over 100 million records worldwide and her career accolades include three Grammy Awards, a Brit Award, a Daytime Emmy Award and seven MTV Video Music Awards.

Tramar Lacel Dillard
September 17, 1979

Rapper, singer, songwriter and composer known professionally as Flo Rida. His 2008 breakout single 'Low' was No.1 for 10 weeks in the U.S. and broke the record for digital download sales at the time of its release. He has since had much international success and had two other U.S. No.1 records, Right Round (2009) and Whistle (2012). Flo Rida has sold over 80 million records worldwide, making him one of the world's best-selling music artists.

Brandon Cole 'Bam' Margera
September 28, 1979

Professional skateboarder, stunt performer, filmmaker, musician and television personality. He came to prominence after appearing as a main cast member in MTV's Jackass. He has since appeared on MTV's Viva La Bam and Bam's Unholy Union, all three Jackass movies, and Haggard: The Movie, and Minghags: The Movie, both of which he co-wrote and directed. In late 2009 Margera released a book containing private writings and pictures entitled Serious as Dog Dirt.

John Burke Krasinski
October 20, 1979

Actor, screenwriter, producer and director. Educated in theatre arts at Brown University and the National Theater Institute, Krasinski played minor roles in movies and off-Broadway plays before he was cast in 2005 as Jim Halpert on the NBC sitcom The Office, a role for which he received critical acclaim. He has received two Primetime Emmy Award nominations and two Screen Actors Guild Awards, and in 2018 Time named him one of the 100 most influential people in the world.

Holly Madison
December 23, 1979

Model, showgirl, television personality and New York Times best-selling author. Madison is known for her role in the E! reality television show, The Girls Next Door and for her own series, Holly's World. In July 2015, Madison released her first book and memoir, Down The Rabbit Hole: Curious Adventures and Cautionary Tales of a Former Playboy Bunny, and in May 2016, released her second book, The Vegas Diaries: Romance, Rolling the Dice, and the Road to Reinvention.

Jan 16	Theodore Crawford Cassidy (b. July 31, 1932) - Radio, television and film actor, and voice artist. Noted for his tall stature (6ft 9in) he is best known for playing the role of Lurch on The Addams Family in the mid-1960s.
Jan 25	Nelson Aldrich Rockefeller (b. July 8, 1908) - Businessman and politician who served as the 41st Vice President of the United States (1974-1977), and previous to that as the 49th Governor of New York (1959-1973).
Mar 28	Emmett Leo Kelly (b. December 9, 1898) - Circus performer who created the memorable clown figure 'Weary Willie'.
May 16	Asa Philip Randolph (b. April 15, 1889) - A leader in the Civil Rights Movement, the American labor movement, and in socialist political parties.
May 29	Mary Pickford (b. Gladys Louise Smith; April 8, 1892) - Film actress and producer whose career spanned 50 years. She was a co-founder of both the Pickford-Fairbanks Studio and the United Artists film studio, and was one of the original 36 founders of the Academy of Motion Picture Arts and Sciences.
Jun 6	John Joseph Haley, Jr. (b. August 10, 1897) - Vaudevillian, actor, radio host, comedian, singer and dancer best known for his portrayal of the Tin Man, and his farmhand counterpart Hickory, in the classic 1939 MGM film The Wizard of Oz.

June 11, 1979: John Wayne (b. Marion Robert Morrison; May 26, 1907) - Actor and filmmaker nicknamed 'The Duke'. Wayne was among the top box office draws for three decades and starred in 142 motion pictures, 83 of them Westerns. He was nominated three times for an Academy Award, winning once for Best Actor for his role as Reuben J. 'Rooster' Cogburn in True Grit (1969) - *pictured left*. Wayne's enduring status as an iconic American was formally recognized by the government in the form of the two highest civilian decorations, the Congressional Gold Medal (1979) and the Presidential Medal of Freedom (1980).

Jul 6	Elizabeth Montague Ryan (b. February 5, 1892) - Tennis player who won 26 Grand Slam titles; nineteen of those titles were in women's doubles and mixed doubles at Wimbledon, an all-time record for those two events.
Jul 6	Van Allen Clinton McCoy (b. January 6, 1940) - Musician, record producer, arranger, songwriter, singer and orchestra conductor who is best known for his 1975 internationally successful song The Hustle.
Jul 12	Minnie Riperton (b. November 8, 1947) - Singer and songwriter best known for her 1975 single Lovin' You, and her four-octave coloratura soprano.

Jul 26	Vivian Vance (b. Vivian Roberta Jones; July 26, 1909) - Television and theater actress and singer. Vance is best known for her role as Ethel Mertz, sidekick to Lucille Ball on the television sitcom I Love Lucy, and as Vivian Bagley on The Lucy Show.
Aug 2	Thurman Lee Munson (b. June 7, 1947) - Professional baseball catcher who played 11 seasons in Major League Baseball for the New York Yankees (1969-1979). A seven-time All-Star, he won the Gold Glove Award in three consecutive years (1973-1975) and was the American League MVP in 1976.
Aug 9	Raymond Lee Washington (b. August 14, 1953) - Gangster and founder of the Crips gang in Los Angeles, California.
Aug 25	Stanley Newcomb Kenton (b. December 15, 1911) - Popular music and jazz artist. As a pianist, composer, arranger and band leader, he led an innovative and influential jazz orchestra for almost four decades.
Sep 2	Otto Paul Weyland (b. January 27, 1903) - U.S. Air Force general and the post-World War II Commander of Far East Air Forces during the Korean War and of Tactical Air Command.
Oct 5	Charlie Smith (b. 1874?) - Centenarian noted for claiming to be the oldest person in the United States. Smith stated that he had been born in Liberia in 1842, making him 137 at the time of his death if true. Later research indicated that he had probably been born circa 1874, making him 105 when he died.

October 15, 1979: Jacob Loucks Devers (b. September 8, 1887) - General in the U.S. Army who commanded the 6th Army Group in the European Theater during World War II. He was involved in the development and adoption of numerous weapons including; the M4 Sherman and M26 Pershing tanks, the DUKW amphibious truck, the Bell H-13 Sioux helicopter and the M16 rifle. *Photo left: Capt. Robert Morgan of the Memphis Belle shaking hands with Gen. Devers before he and the crew returned to the U.S. (having completed 25 combat missions).*

Nov 1	Mamie Geneva Doud Eisenhower (b. November 14, 1896) - Wife of President Dwight D. Eisenhower and the First Lady from 1953 to 1961.
Nov 5	Al Capp (b. Alfred Gerald Caplin; September 28, 1909) - Cartoonist and humorist best known for the satirical comic strip Li'l Abner.
Nov 30	Herbert Manfred 'Zeppo' Marx (b. February 25, 1901) - Actor, comedian, theatrical agent, and engineer who was the youngest of the five Marx Brothers. He appeared in the first five Marx Brothers feature films, from 1929 to 1933, but then left the act to start his second career as an engineer and theatrical agent.
Dec 25	Rose Joan Blondell (b. August 30, 1906) - Actress who began her career in vaudeville and performed in movies and on television for half a century. She was nominated for an Oscar for Best Supporting Actress in The Blue Veil (1951).
Dec 30	Richard Charles Rodgers (b. June 28, 1902) - One of the most significant composers of 20th century American music. Rodgers is best known for his song writing partnerships with the lyricists Lorenz Hart and Oscar Hammerstein II.

1979 TOP 10 SINGLES

No.1	My Sharona - *The Knack*
No.2	Bad Girls - *Donna Summer*
No.3	Le Freak - *Chic*
No.4	Da Ya Think I'm Sexy? - *Rod Stewart*
No.5	Reunited - *Peaches & Herb*
No.6	I Will Survive - *Gloria Gaynor*
No.7	Hot Stuff - *Donna Summer*
No.8	Y.M.C.A. - *Village People*
No.9	Ring My Bell - *Anita Ward*
No.10	Sad Eyes - *Robert John*

① **The Knack**
My Sharona

Label:	Written by:	Length:
Capitol Records	Averre / Fieger	3 mins 58 secs

The Knack was a rock band based in Los Angeles that rose to fame with their debut single, 'My Sharona'. The song was written by Berton Averre and Doug Fieger, and was released in 1979 from their album Get the Knack. It reached No.1 on the Billboard Hot 100 singles chart, where it remained for 6 weeks, and was certified gold (more than 1 million records sold) by the Recording Industry Association of America. 'My Sharona' was Capitol Records' fastest gold status debut single since the Beatles' 'I Want to Hold Your Hand' in 1964.

② **Donna Summer**
Bad Girls

Label:	Written by:	Length:
Casablanca	Sudano / Summer	4 mins 55 secs

Donna Summer (b. LaDonna Adrian Gaines; December 31, 1948 - d. May 17, 2012) was a singer, songwriter and painter who gained prominence during the disco era of the late-1970s. 'Bad Girls' is a song from her seventh studio album of the same name, and was released on June 23, 1979, through Casablanca Records. The single became a worldwide success, peaking within the top-ten in seven countries, and helped the Bad Girls album to reach multi-platinum status in the U.S.

③ Chic
Le Freak

Label:	Written by:	Length:
Atlantic	Rodgers / Edwards	3 mins 30 secs

Chic, currently called Nile Rodgers & Chic, was formed by guitarist Nile Rodgers and bassist Bernard Edwards in 1976. The group regarded themselves as a rock band for the disco movement "that made good on hippie peace, love and freedom". The song 'Le Freak' was the band's third single and their first Billboard Hot 100 and R&B No.1 - it went on to achieve sales of 7 million worldwide. In 2017 Chic was nominated for induction into the Rock and Roll Hall of Fame for the eleventh time.

---

④ Rod Stewart
Da Ya Think I'm Sexy?

Label:	Written by:	Length:
Warner Bros. Records	Appice / Stewart	5 mins 28 secs

Sir Roderick David Stewart, CBE (b. January 10, 1945) is a British rock singer and songwriter who is one of the best-selling music artists of all time having sold over 100 million records worldwide. Stewart was sued by Brazilian singer Jorge Ben over the rights to 'Da Ya Think I'm Sexy?' claiming the tune was too similar to his work, 'Taj Mahal'. Ben won and then asked him to donate all his publishing royalties from the record to UNICEF. Stewart has been inducted twice into the Rock and Roll Hall of Fame; in 1994 as a solo artist, and in 2012 as a member of the rock band Faces.

⑤ Peaches & Herb
Reunited

Label:	Written by:	Length:
Polydor	Fekaris / Perren	3 mins 58 secs

Peaches & Herb are a vocalist duo. Herb Fame (b. October 1, 1942) has remained a constant since the duo was created in 1966 but seven different women have filled the role of "Peaches", including Linda Greene (the third Peaches) who appeared on the duo's biggest hits 'Shake Your Groove Thing' (1978) and 'Reunited' (1979). 'Reunited' was the second single released from their 1978 album, 2 Hot, and was a huge crossover smash, topping both the pop and soul charts.

---

⑥ Gloria Gaynor
I Will Survive

Label:	Written by:	Length:
Polydor	Fekaris / Perren	3 mins 15 secs

Gloria Gaynor (b. Gloria Fowles; September 7, 1949) is a singer best known for the disco era hits 'I Will Survive' and 'Never Can Say Goodbye' (1974). 'I Will Survive' was originally released as the B-side to a cover version of the Righteous Brothers song 'Substitute' but became a worldwide hit for Gaynor when disc jockeys decided to play it instead of the A-side. It went on to sell over 14 million copies worldwide and has remained a popular disco anthem ever since.

7 Donna Summer
Hot Stuff

Label:	Written by:	Length:
Casablanca	Faltermeyer / Forsey / Bellotte	6 mins 45 secs

Donna Summer's 'Hot Stuff' was the lead single from her seventh studio album Bad Girls (1979) and won her the Grammy Award for Best Female Rock Vocal Performance in its inaugural year. Up to that point Summer had mainly been associated with disco songs but this song also showed a significant rock direction, including a guitar solo by ex-Doobie Brother and Steely Dan guitarist Jeff "Skunk" Baxter. Summer earned a total of 42 hit singles on the U.S. Billboard Hot 100 in her lifetime, won five Grammy Awards and sold over 140 million records worldwide.

---

8 Village People
Y.M.C.A.

Label:	Written by:	Length:
Casablanca	Belolo / Willis / Morali	3 mins 30 secs

Village People is a disco group best known for their on-stage costumes, catchy tunes, and suggestive lyrics. The group was originally formed by French producers Jacques Morali, Henri Belolo and lead singer Victor Willis following the release of the debut album, Village People, which targeted disco's gay audience. The group quickly became popular and moved into the mainstream scoring several hits internationally including the hit singles 'Macho Man', 'In the Navy', 'Go West' and their biggest hit, 'Y.M.C.A.'.

9 Anita Ward
Ring My Bell

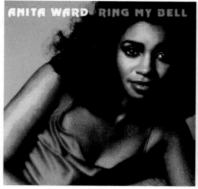  

Label:	**Written by:**	**Length:**
T.K. Disco	Frederick Knight	8 mins 8 secs

Anita Ward (b. December 20, 1957) is a singer and musician who is best known for her 1979 million selling chart-topper 'Ring My Bell'. The song was originally written for the then eleven-year-old Stacy Lattisaw (by Frederick Knight) as a teenybopper song about kids talking on the telephone. When Lattisaw signed for a different label Ward was asked to sing it instead and it became her only major hit when it went to No.1 on both the Billboard Hot 100 chart and the Soul Singles chart. It also garnered Ward a nomination for Best Female R&B Vocal Performance at the 1980 Grammy Awards.

10 Robert John
Sad Eyes

Label:	**Written by:**	**Length:**
EMI America	Robert John	3 mins 30 secs

Robert John (b. Robert John Pedrick, Jr.; January 3, 1946) is a singer-songwriter who first hit the pop chart in 1958 when he was only 12 years old with 'White Bucks and Saddle Shoes'. He is probably best known though for his hit single, 'Sad Eyes', which was released in April 1979 and eventually reached the top of the chart 6 months later on October 6. 'Sad Eyes' is one of only a few non-disco, or disco-influenced, songs to top the 1979 pop chart.

1979: TOP FILMS

1. **Kramer vs. Kramer** - *Columbia*
2. **The Amityville Horror** - *American International Pictures*
3. **Rocky II** - *United Artists*
4. **Apocalypse Now** - *United Artists*
5. **Star Trek: The Motion Picture** - *Paramount*

OSCARS

Best Picture: Kramer vs. Kramer

Most Nominations: All That Jazz and Kramer vs. Kramer (9)
Most Wins: Kramer vs. Kramer (5)

Best Director: Robert Benton - *Kramer vs. Kramer*

Best Actor: Dustin Hoffman - *Kramer vs. Kramer*
Best Actress: Sally Field - *Norma Rae*
Best Supporting Actor: Melvyn Douglas - *Being There*
Best Supporting Actress: Meryl Streep - *Kramer vs. Kramer*

The 52nd Academy Awards were presented on April 14, 1980.

Directed by: Robert Benton - Runtime: 1 hour 45 minutes

Ted Kramer's wife Joanna leaves him allowing for a lost bond to be rediscovered between Ted and his son Billy. A heated battle then ensues over Billy as Ted and Joanna go to court to fight for custody of their son.

STARRING

Dustin Hoffman
Born: August 8, 1937

Character:
Ted Kramer

Actor and director with a career in film, television and theatre since 1960. His breakthrough film role came in 1967 when he played the title character Benjamin Braddock in the The Graduate. Hoffman has been nominated for seven Academy Awards, winning twice for Best Actor in Kramer vs. Kramer (1979) and Rain Man (1988). He has also won six Golden Globes (including an honorary one) and four BAFTAs.

Meryl Streep
Born: June 22, 1949

Character:
Joanna Kramer

Actress born Mary Louise Streep who is often described as the 'best actress of her generation'. Nominated for a record 21 Academy Awards, she has won three. Streep has received 31 Golden Globe nominations, winning eight - more nominations and wins than any other actor. She has also won three Primetime Emmy Awards and has been nominated for fifteen British Academy Film Awards, and seventeen Screen Actors Guild Awards, winning two of each.

Jane Alexander
Born: October 28, 1939

Character:
Margaret Phelps

Author, actress, and former director of the National Endowment for the Arts. Alexander made her Broadway debut in 1968 in The Great White Hope and won the 1969 Tony Award for Best Featured Actress in a Play. In total she has received seven Tony Award nominations and was inducted into the American Theater Hall of Fame in 1994. In film she has received four Academy Award nominations for her performances; Kramer vs. Kramer earned her her third nomination.

TRIVIA

Goofs	Ted Kramer's lawyer tells him that if he wishes to appeal the decision granting custody to his ex-wife his son would have to take the stand. On an appeal no new evidence is called upon and therefore the son would not be called as a witness.
	The trees are green in the scenes which supposedly take place in New York at Halloween and Christmas.
Interesting Facts	Meryl Streep wrote her own courtroom speech upon writer and director Robert Benton's suggestion after she told him she wasn't satisfied with the way it was originally written.

CONTINUED

Interesting Facts

The strength of the performances of the two leads can be at least partly attributed to what was going on in their private lives at the time. Hoffman was in the midst of a messy divorce while Streep was still recovering from the death of her lover John Cazale.

Dustin Hoffman planned the moment when he throws his wine glass against the wall during the restaurant scene with Meryl Streep. The only person he warned in advance was the cameraman, to make sure that it got in the shot. Streep's shocked reaction was real, but she stayed in character long enough for writer and director Robert Benton to yell cut. In the documentary on the DVD she recalls yelling at Hoffman as soon as the shot was over for scaring her so badly.

Meryl Streep left her just-claimed Oscar for the film on the back of a toilet during the 1980 festivities.

When Justin Henry, who played the Kramer's son Billy, was nominated for the Academy Award for Best Actor in a Supporting Role, Henry, at the age of eight, became the youngest person to be nominated for this award, as well as the youngest Oscar nominee in any category, a record which still stands today.

Quote

Billy Kramer: When's Mommy coming back?
Ted Kramer: I dont know, Billy. Soon.
Billy Kramer: How soon?
Ted Kramer: Soon.
Billy Kramer: Will she pick me up after school?
Ted Kramer: Probably. And if she doesn't I will.
Billy Kramer: What if you forget?
Ted Kramer: I won't forget.
Billy Kramer: What if you get run over by a truck and get killed?
Ted Kramer: Then Mommy will pick you up.

THE AMITYVILLE HORROR

Directed by: Stuart Rosenberg - Runtime: 1 hour 57 minutes

Newlyweds move into a large house where a mass murder was committed and experience strange manifestations which drive them away.

STARRING

James Brolin
Born: July 18, 1940

Character:
George Lutz

Actor, producer and director born Craig Kenneth Bruderlin. He is best known for his roles in film and television, including sitcoms and soap operas - he is currently playing the role of John, the family patriarch, in the CBS comedy Life in Pieces. He is the father of actor Josh Brolin and husband of Barbra Streisand. Brolin has won two Golden Globes and an Emmy, and received a star on the Hollywood Walk of Fame on August 10, 2016.

Margot Kidder
Born: October 17, 1948
Died: May 13, 2018

Character:
Kathy Lutz

A Canadian-American actress and activist whose career spanned over five decades. She started out in the 1960s appearing in low-budget Canadian films and television series before landing a lead role in Quackser Fortune Has a Cousin in the Bronx (1970). Her accolades include three Canadian Screen Awards and one Daytime Emmy Award. Kidder is most widely known for her performances as Lois Lane in the Superman film series.

Rod Steiger
Born: April 14, 1925
Died: July 9, 2002

Character:
Father Delaney

Actor noted for his portrayal of offbeat, often volatile and crazed characters. He made his film debut in Teresa (1951), and subsequently appeared in films such as Oklahoma! (1955), Across the Bridge (1957) and Al Capone (1959). Other notable roles include starring as Marlon Brando's mobster brother Charley in On the Waterfront (1954), Sol Nazerman in The Pawnbroker (1964), and Bill Gillespie (opposite Sidney Poitier) in In the Heat of the Night (1967), which won him the Academy Award for Best Actor.

TRIVIA

Goofs	When the cheek-pinching Aunt Helena arrives (at around 36 mins), Matthew answers the door with a very red left cheek from a previous take.
	Toward the end of the film lightning smashes through one of the attic windows (during the axe attack), but subsequent exterior shots (the escape) show both windows still intact.
Interesting Facts	At the time of its release the film was one of the highest grossing independent films of all time, and was American International Pictures' biggest hit.

Interesting Facts

James Brolin was hesitant when he was first offered the role of George Lutz. He was told that there was no script and that he must obtain a copy of Jay Anson's novel and read it as soon as possible. Brolin started the book one evening at seven o'clock and was still reading at two o'clock in the morning. He had hung a pair of his pants up in the room earlier and at a really tense part in the book the pants fell down unexpectedly, causing Brolin to jump out of his chair and nearly hit his head on the ceiling. It was then that Brolin thought, "there's something to this story" and agreed to do the movie.

While shooting the scene where Kathy Lutz is startled by the red eyes in the window, director Stuart Rosenberg wasn't impressed by Margot Kidder's reaction. According to Kidder, Rosenberg then tried to hold up a "a day-glo orange stuffed velour pig with glass eyes" in an attempt to startle her. The result, far from frightening her, was merely hysterical laughter.

As the movie was made on a relatively modest budget James Brolin took less money up front and agreed to take 10% of the gross sales after its release. After the film became an unexpected blockbuster (at that time it was in the top ten of all time), he eventually received about $17 million - if adjusted for inflation that would be equivalent to a little over $59 million as of 2018.

In hopes of creating more publicity for the film the studio concocted stories of "weird" occurrences on the set of the film.

Due to all the unwanted fame the book and film had brought upon the real house in Amityville, the current owners have replaced the "evil eyes" windows with normal rectangle-shaped windows.

Quotes

Kathy Lutz: I just wish that... all those people hadn't died here. I mean... ugh! A guy kills his whole family. Doesn't that bother you?
George Lutz: Well, sure, but... houses don't have memories.

The House: GET OUT!

ROCKY II

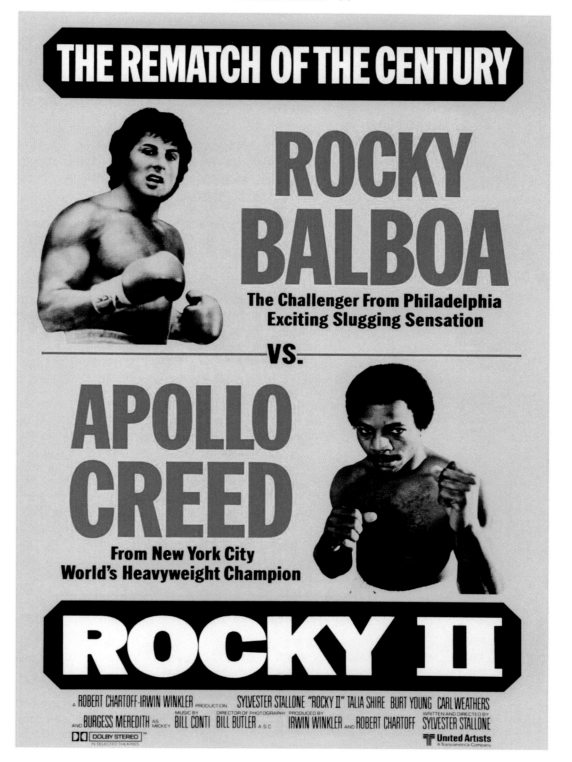

THE REMATCH OF THE CENTURY

ROCKY BALBOA
The Challenger From Philadelphia
Exciting Slugging Sensation

VS.

APOLLO CREED
From New York City
World's Heavyweight Champion

ROCKY II

A ROBERT CHARTOFF-IRWIN WINKLER PRODUCTION   SYLVESTER STALLONE "ROCKY II" TALIA SHIRE BURT YOUNG   CARL WEATHERS
AND BURGESS MEREDITH AS MICKEY   MUSIC BY BILL CONTI DIRECTOR OF PHOTOGRAPHY BILL BUTLER A.S.C.   PRODUCED BY IRWIN WINKLER AND ROBERT CHARTOFF   WRITTEN AND DIRECTED BY SYLVESTER STALLONE
DOLBY STEREO IN SELECTED THEATRES   United Artists A Transamerica Company

Directed by: Sylvester Stallone - Runtime: 1 hour 59 minutes

Rocky runs into financial and family problems after his bout with Apollo Creed. The embarrassed champ meanwhile goads him into getting back in the ring for a rematch.

STARRING

Sylvester Stallone
Born: July 6, 1946

Character:
Rocky Balboa

Actor, screenwriter, producer and director. Stallone is well known for his Hollywood action roles, in particular as boxer Rocky Balboa in the Rocky series of seven films (1976-2015), but also as soldier John Rambo from the four Rambo films (1982-2008) and Barney Ross in the three The Expendables movies (2010-2014). Stallone wrote or co-wrote most of the 14 films in all three franchises and also directed many of them.

Talia Shire
Born: April 25, 1946

Characters:
Adrian

Actress who first became famous for her role of Connie Corleone in The Godfather and its sequels, for which she was nominated for the Academy Award for Best Supporting Actress in The Godfather: Part II. In Rocky she portrayed Adrian Pennino Balboa and was nominated for a second Academy Award for Best Actress. She has also starred in films such as Kiss the Bride (2002), I ♥ Huckabees (2004) and Homo Erectus (2007).

Burt Young
Born: April 30, 1940

Character:
Paulie

Actor, painter and author born Gerald Tommaso DeLouise. He is best known for his Academy Award-nominated role as Sylvester Stallone's brother-in-law and best friend Paulie Pennino in the Rocky film series. As a painter Young's art has been displayed in galleries throughout the world and as a published author his works include two filmed screenplays and a 400-page historically based novel called Endings.

TRIVIA

Goofs | It's well established that Rocky is left handed, however when he signs an autograph for the nurse at the beginning of the movie he uses his right hand.

When Adrian is in a coma, Rocky's facial hair is used to give a general idea of time. Just before Adrian comes out of the coma you can see Rocky with almost a full beard. The shot pans over to Adrian opening her eyes. When the shot pans back to Rocky he barely has a 5 o'clock shadow.

Interesting Facts | When Rocky is training for the fight he is sparring with a smaller quicker fighter, the sparring partner is played by real life Champion Roberto Durán.

CONTINUED

Interesting Facts

Analysis by Philadelphia locals tracked the route Rocky took through the city during his training run (when all the children joined him). If he took this actual route from his South Philly house to the top of the Art Museum steps, he would have covered approximately 30 miles!

During his preparation for the film Sylvester Stallone was bench-pressing 220 pounds when the weight fell and tore his right pectoral muscle. This was shortly before the final fight scene was to be filmed and ultimately led to the scene being shot with Stallone still badly injured.

Originally Adrian was supposed to be at the big fight, however, because Talia Shire was working on another movie at the time the storyline was changed to having her stay home and watch the fight on television. The scenes of her watching the boxing match on television were shot and then edited into the movie several months after filming had finished.

It took Sylvester Stallone and editors Danford B. Greene and Stanford C. Allen over eight months to edit the climatic fight scene so as to meet Stallone's approval.

Stallone began working on the Rocky III (1982) script immediately after completing Rocky II, with the intention of the series being a trilogy - he had no intention of making any further Rocky films.

Quotes

[Mickey has Rocky chase after a chicken as part of his training]
Rocky Balboa: I feel like a Kentucky Fried idiot.

Rocky Balboa: *[After round 1 of the rematch with Creed]* I can't believe it!
Mickey: What?
Rocky Balboa: He broke my nose again.

Rocky Balboa: I just got one thing to say... to my wife at home: Yo, Adrian! I DID IT!

APOCALYPSE NOW

Directed by: Francis Ford Coppola - Runtime: 2 hours 27 minutes

During the Vietnam War, Captain Willard is sent on a dangerous mission into Cambodia to assassinate a renegade Colonel who has set himself up as a god among a local tribe.

STARRING

Marlon Brando
Born: April 3, 1924
Died: July 1, 2004

Character:
Colonel Walter E. Kurtz

Actor, film director and activist. He is credited with bringing a gripping realism to film acting and is often cited as one of the greatest and most influential actors of all time. He helped to popularise the Stanislavski system of acting, today more commonly referred to as method acting. Brando is most famous for his Academy Award-winning performances as Terry Malloy in On the Waterfront (1954) and Vito Corleone in The Godfather (1972).

Martin Sheen
Born: August 3, 1940

Character:
Captain Benjamin L.
Willard

American-Irish actor, born Ramón Gerard Antonio Estévez, who first became known for his roles in the films The Subject Was Roses (1968) and Badlands (1973). He later achieved wide recognition for his leading role in Apocalypse Now (1979) and as President Josiah Bartlet in the television series The West Wing (1999-2006). Sheen received a star on the Hollywood Walk of Fame in 1989 and is the father of four children, all of whom are actors.

Robert Duvall
Born: January 5, 1931

Character:
Lieutenant Colonel Bill
Kilgore

Actor and filmmaker whose career spans more than six decades. Duvall began appearing in theatre during the late 1950s, moving into television and film roles during the early 1960s. He has been nominated for seven Academy Awards, winning once for his performance in Tender Mercies (1983), seven Golden Globe Awards (winning four), and has multiple nominations and one win each of the BAFTA, Screen Actors Guild Award, and Emmy Award.

TRIVIA

Goofs	During Willard's briefing in Nha Trang, every time someone mentions the name "Kurtz" on the soundtrack, on screen they are mouthing "Lieghley", the original name of Col. Kurtz's character in the script during the early part of the shooting.
	After the canopy of the boat is destroyed and is replaced by giant leaves, it reappears again when they are at the bridge. In subsequent shots it is again replaced by leaves.
Interesting Facts	Laurence Fishburne, who plays Tyrone 'Clean' Miller, was 14 when production began in 1976. He lied about his age.

CONTINUED

Interesting Facts

There are no opening credits or titles. The title appears late in the film as graffiti which reads "Our motto: Apocalypse Now". The film could not be copyrighted as "Apocalypse Now" unless the title was seen in the film.

Francis Ford Coppola shot nearly 200 hours of footage during the making of this film.

Most of the dialogue was added in post-production. Extraneous noise such as helicopters left many scenes with unusable audio.

It took Francis Ford Coppola nearly three years to edit the footage. While working on his final edit it became apparent to him that Martin Sheen would be needed to tape several additional narrative voice-overs. Coppola soon discovered that Sheen was busy and unable to perform these voice-overs. He then called in Sheen's brother, Joe Estevez, whose voice sounded nearly identical, to perform the new narrative tracks. Estevez was also used as a stand-in when Sheen suffered a heart attack during the shoot in 1976. Estevez was not credited for his work as a stand-in, nor for his voice-over work.

Robert Duvall's iconic Oscar-nominated performance as Colonel Kilgore amounts to just eleven minutes of screentime.

Quotes

[While flying in a helicopter with Air Cavalry soldiers]
Chef: Why do all you guys sit on your helmets?
Door Gunner: So we don't get our balls blown off.

Kilgore: I love the smell of napalm in the morning.

STAR TREK: THE MOTION PICTURE

Directed by: Robert Wise - Runtime: 2 hours 12 minutes

When an alien spacecraft of enormous power is spotted approaching Earth, Admiral James T. Kirk resumes command of the overhauled USS Enterprise in order to intercept it.

STARRING

William Shatner
Born: March 22, 1931

Character:
Captain James T. Kirk

Canadian actor, author, producer, director and singer. In his seven decades of television Shatner has become a cultural icon for his portrayal of James T. Kirk, captain of the USS Enterprise, in the Star Trek franchise. Other notable television appearances include playing the eponymous veteran police sergeant in T.J. Hooker (1982-1986) and hosting Rescue 911 (1989-1996), which won a People's Choice Award for the Favorite New TV Dramatic Series.

Leonard Nimoy
Born: March 26, 1931
Died: February 27, 2015

Character:
Commander Spock

Actor, film director, photographer, author, singer and songwriter. Nimoy began his career in his early twenties teaching acting classes in Hollywood, and making minor film and television appearances throughout the 1950s. He was best known though for his role as Spock of the Star Trek franchise, a character he portrayed in television and film from a pilot episode shot in late 1964 to his final film performance in 2013.

DeForest Kelley
Born: January 20, 1920
Died: June 11, 1999

Character:
Dr. McCoy

Actor, screenwriter, poet and singer. During World War II, Kelley served as an enlisted man in the U.S. Army Air Forces assigned to the First Motion Picture Unit. His acting career began with the feature film Fear in the Night (1947), a low-budget movie that brought him to the attention of a national audience. He was best known for his roles in Westerns and as Dr. Leonard 'Bones' McCoy of the USS Enterprise in the television and film series Star Trek.

TRIVIA

Goofs	In the Original Star Trek Series Spock says that the planet Vulcan has no Moon, but while he is meditating on Vulcan in this film, a Moon can be seen. This anomaly has been fixed in the 'Director's Edition' of the movie with the Moon being removed, and the addition of an actual atmosphere and sky on Vulcan.
	William Shatner's hairstyle appears to change in nearly every scene.
Interesting Facts	The cast hated the uniforms which required assistance in order to be removed. In fact one of the cast's conditions for returning in a sequel was that they have new uniforms.

CONTINUED

Interesting Facts

The Klingon words spoken by the Klingon captain were actually invented by James Doohan (Commander Scott). Linguist Marc Okrand later devised grammar and syntax rules for the language, along with more vocabulary words in Star Trek III: The Search for Spock (1984), and wrote a Klingon dictionary. He based all his work on those few Klingon lines in this movie so that they made sense retrospectively.

Persis Khambatta became very emotional about having her head shaved for her role as Lieutenant Ilia. She kept her shorn hair in a box for a time and asked Gene Roddenberry to take out insurance in case her hair did not grow back. It did.

Uhura's communications earpieces are the only props from the original Star Trek (1966) series. They were dug out of storage when it was realized someone had forgotten to make new ones for the movie.

The producers and the cast were very worried about their appearances after being away from Star Trek for ten years. Special lighting and camera tricks were used to hide the cast's aging, and William Shatner went on a near-starvation diet prior to filming. However, in all subsequent Star Trek movies it was decided to make the aging of the crew part of the story.

Quotes

Dr. McCoy: Spock, you haven't changed a bit. You're just as warm and sociable as ever.
Commander Spock: Nor have you, doctor, as your continued predilection for irrelevancy demonstrates.

Captain Kirk: Well, for a man who swore he'd never return to the Starfleet...
Dr. McCoy: Just a moment, Captain, sir. I'll explain what happened. Your revered Admiral Nogura invoked a little-known, seldom-used 'reserve activation clause'. In simpler language, Captain, they DRAFTED me!
Captain Kirk: *[in mock horror]* They didn't.
Dr. McCoy: This was your idea. This was your idea, wasn't it?

SPORTING WINNERS

WILLIE STARGELL - MAJOR LEAGUE BASEBALL

 Associated Press - MALE ATHLETE OF THE YEAR

Wilver Dornell Stargell
Born: March 6, 1940 - Earlsboro, Oklahoma
Died: April 9, 2001 - Wilmington, North Carolina
MLB debut: September 16, 1962, for the Pittsburgh Pirates
Last MLB appearance: October 3, 1982, for the Pittsburgh Pirates

Willie Stargell, nicknamed "Pops" in the later years of his career, was a professional baseball player who played his entire Major League Baseball career as the left fielder and first baseman for the Pittsburgh Pirates of the National League. Over his 21-year career with the Pirates he batted .282, with 2,232 hits, 423 doubles, 475 home runs, and 1,540 runs batted in, helping his team capture six NL East division titles, two National League pennants, and two World Series.

Career Highlights / Awards:

All-Star	1964-1966, 1971-1973, 1978
World Series Champion	1971, 1979
NL MVP	1979
World Series MVP	1979
NLCS MVP	1979
Roberto Clemente Award	1974
NL Home Run Leader	1971, 1973
NL RBI Leader	1973
Pittsburgh Pirates No.8	Retired

The Pirates retired Stargell's number 8 on September 6, 1982 and he was inducted into the Baseball Hall of Fame in 1988 (vote: 82.4% - first ballot). After Stargell died in 2001, Joe Morgan said, "When I played, there were 600 baseball players, and 599 of them loved Willie Stargell. He's the only guy I could have said that about. He never made anybody look bad and he never said anything bad about anybody".

TRACY AUSTIN - TENNIS

 **Associated Press** - FEMALE ATHLETE OF THE YEAR

Tracy Ann Austin Holt
Born: December 12, 1962 - Palos Verdes Peninsula, California
Turned Professional: October 23, 1978 / Retired: July 1994
Highest ranking - No.1 (April 7, 1980)
Career Prize Money: $1,992,380

Tracy Austin is a former World No.1 professional tennis player. She won three Grand Slam titles, the WTA Tour Championships in 1980, and the year-ending Toyota Championships in 1981. In 1979 she became the youngest U.S. Open female singles champion in history (aged 16 years and 9 months), and she is the youngest inductee of all time at the International Tennis Hall of Fame. Austin won singles titles on all playing surfaces: clay (both red clay and green clay), indoor carpet, grass, and hard courts.

Tennis Titles:

Grand Slam Singles	U.S. Open	1979, 1981
Grand Slam Doubles	Wimbledon	1980
Team Competitions	Federation Cup	1978, 1979, 1980

Career record: 335-90 (78.82%) / Career titles: 30

A series of injuries and a serious automobile accident cut short her career. Since retiring as a player Austin has worked as a commentator for NBC and the USA Network, for the French Open and the U.S. Open. She has also worked for the Seven Network, who broadcast the Australian Open, the BBC for Wimbledon, and Canadian television for their coverage of the Rogers Cup.

GOLF

THE MASTERS - FUZZY ZOELLER

The Masters Tournament is the first of the majors to be played each year and unlike the other major championships it is played at the same location, Augusta National Golf Club, Georgia. This was the 43rd Masters Tournament and was held April 12-15. Fuzzy Zoeller won his only Masters with a birdie on the second hole of a playoff with Ed Sneed and Tom Watson. It was the first of Zoeller's two major titles and earned him a $50,000 share of the prize fund.

U.S. OPEN - HALE IRWIN

The 1979 U.S. Open Championship (established in 1895) was held June 14-17 at Inverness Club in Toledo, Ohio. Hale Irwin won the second of three U.S. Open titles (he also won in 1974 and 1990), two strokes ahead of former champions Jerry Pate and Gary Player. Irwin's share of the prize fund was $50,000.

PGA CHAMPIONSHIP - DAVID GRAHAM

The 1979 and 61st PGA Championship was played August 2-5 at Oakland Hills Country Club in Bloomfield Township, Michigan, a suburb northwest of Detroit. David Graham won the first of his two major titles on the third hole of a sudden-death playoff with Ben Crenshaw. Through 17 holes in the final round Graham was seven-under, with seven birdies and ten pars. Of the 21 holes he played Sunday, nine were birdies. The total prize fund for the Championship was $350,600 of which $60,000 went to the champion Graham.

Hale Irwin

David Graham

Fuzzy Zoeller

54

WORLD SERIES - PITTSBURGH PIRATES

Pittsburgh Pirates

4 - 3

Baltimore Orioles

Total attendance: 367,597 - Average attendance: 52,514
Winning player's share: $28,264 - Losing player's share: $22,114

The World Series is the annual championship series of Major League Baseball played since 1903 between the American League and the National League champion teams. It is determined through a best-of-seven playoff.

The 1979 World Series saw the National League champions, the Pittsburgh Pirates, beating the American League champions, the Baltimore Orioles, by four games to three. The Pirates became the fourth team in World Series history to come back from a three games to one deficit to win the Series in seven games.

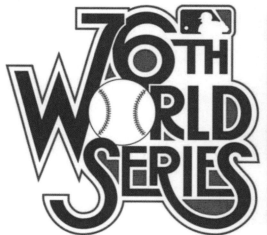

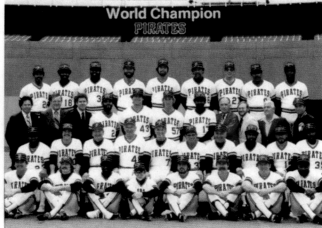

The 76th World Series Champions the Pittsburgh Pirates.

	Date	Score			Location	Time	Att.
1	Oct 10	Pirates	4-5	**Orioles**	Memorial Stadium	3:18	53,735
2	Oct 11	**Pirates**	3-2	Orioles	Memorial Stadium	3:13	53,739
3	Oct 12	**Orioles**	8-4	Pirates	Three Rivers Stadium	2:51	50,848
4	Oct 13	**Orioles**	9-6	Pirates	Three Rivers Stadium	3:48	50,883
5	Oct 14	Orioles	1-7	**Pirates**	Three Rivers Stadium	2:54	50,920
6	Oct 16	**Pirates**	4-0	Orioles	Memorial Stadium	2:30	53,739
7	Oct 17	**Pirates**	4-1	Orioles	Memorial Stadium	2:54	53,733

Horse Racing

Spectacular Bid, ridden by 19-year old Ronnie Franklin, takes the 1979 Kentucky Derby.

Spectacular Bid (February 17, 1976 - June 9, 2003) was an American Hall of Fame Champion Thoroughbred racehorse who was owned by Hawksworth Farm and trained by future Hall of Famer Bud Delp. Spectacular Bid was the leading colt of his generation and was voted American Champion Colt in both 1978 and 1979, and American Horse of the Year in 1980. In the 1979 Classic races he won both the Kentucky Derby and Preakness stakes, before sustaining a controversial defeat in the Belmont Stakes (he stepped on a safety pin on the morning of the race and the pin became embedded in his hoof). During his racing career Spectacular Bid won 26 of 30 races, set several track records and earned $2,781,607, a then-record sum.

Kentucky Derby - Spectacular Bid

The Kentucky Derby is held annually at Churchill Downs in Louisville, Kentucky on the first Saturday in May. The race is a Grade 1 stakes race for three-year-olds and is one and a quarter mile in length.

Preakness Stakes - Spectacular Bid

The Preakness Stakes is held on the third Saturday in May each year at Pimlico Race Course in Baltimore, Maryland. It is a Grade 1 race run over a distance of 9½ furlongs (1 3/16 miles) on dirt.

Belmont Stakes - Coastal

The Belmont Stakes is Grade 1 race held every June at Belmont Park in Elmont, New York. It is 1½ miles in length and open to three-year-old thoroughbreds. It takes place on a Saturday between June 5 and June 11.

AMERICAN FOOTBALL

19 - 31

Los Angeles Rams
NFC

Pittsburgh Steelers
AFC

Played: January 20, 1980 at the Rose Bowl, Pasadena, California
MVP: Terry Bradshaw, Quarterback (Pittsburgh Steelers)
Referee: Fred Silva - Attendance: 103,985

The 1979 NFL season was the 60th regular season of the National Football League. The season ended with Super Bowl XIV when the Pittsburgh Steelers repeated as champions by defeating the Los Angeles Rams 31-19 at the Rose Bowl (and thus became the first team to win back-to-back Super Bowls twice).

AMERICAN FOOTBALL CONFERENCE

Division	Team	P	W	L	T	PCT	PF	PA
Eastern Division	Miami Dolphins	16	10	6	0	.625	341	257
Central Division	Pittsburgh Steelers	16	12	4	0	.750	416	262
Western Division	San Diego Chargers	16	12	4	0	.750	411	246

AFC Championship Game: Pittsburgh Steelers 27-13 Houston Oilers

NATIONAL FOOTBALL CONFERENCE

Division	Team	P	W	L	T	PCT	PF	PA
Eastern Division	Dallas Cowboys	16	11	5	0	.688	371	313
Central Division	Tampa Bay Buccaneers	16	10	6	0	.625	273	237
Western Division	Los Angeles Rams	16	9	7	0	.563	323	309

NFC Championship Game: Los Angeles Rams 9-0 Tampa Bay Buccaneers

NHL FINALS - STANLEY CUP

4 - 1

Montreal Canadiens   **New York Rangers**

Series Summary:

	Date	Road Team	Result	Home Team
1	May 13	**New York Rangers**	4-1	Montreal Canadiens
2	May 15	New York Rangers	2-6	**Montreal Canadiens**
3	May 17	**Montreal Canadiens**	4-1	New York Rangers
4	May 19	**Montreal Canadiens**	4-3	New York Rangers
5	May 21	New York Rangers	1-4	**Montreal Canadiens**

The 1979 Stanley Cup Finals was the championship series of the National Hockey League's 1978-1979 season, and the culmination of the 1979 Stanley Cup playoffs. It was contested between the New York Rangers and the defending champions the Montreal Canadiens. The Canadiens won the best-of-seven series four games to one to win their fourth consecutive Stanley Cup championship. The MVP was Bob Gainey (Canadiens).

BASKETBALL - NBA FINALS

4 - 1

Seattle SuperSonics   **Washington Bullets**

Series Summary:

	Date	Home Team	Result	Road Team
1	May 20	**Washington Bullets**	99-97	Seattle SuperSonics
2	May 24	Washington Bullets	82-92	**Seattle SuperSonics**
3	May 27	**Seattle SuperSonics**	105-95	Washington Bullets
4	May 29	**Seattle SuperSonics**	114-112	Washington Bullets
5	Jun 1	Washington Bullets	93-97	**Seattle SuperSonics**

The 1979 NBA World Championship Series was the conclusion of the National Basketball Association 1978-1979 season. The Western Conference champions, Seattle SuperSonics, played the Eastern Conference champions, Washington Bullets, with the Bullets holding home-court advantage due to a better regular season record. The SuperSonics defeated the Bullets 4-1 to win their only Championship. The MVP was Dennis Johnson (Seattle SuperSonics).

INDIANAPOLIS 500 - RICK MEARS

Rick Mears with his Indy 500 winning Gould Garage Penske/Cosworth.

The 63rd International 500-Mile Sweepstakes Race was held at the Indianapolis Motor Speedway on Sunday May 27, 1979, and was won by Rick Mears in front of an estimated crowd of 350,000 spectators. Mears took the lead for the final time with 18 laps to go and won his first of four Indianapolis 500 races - he would win the race again in 1984, 1988 and 1991. Notably it was also Mears' first of a record six Indy 500 pole positions.

BOSTON MARATHON
BILL RODGERS

The Boston Marathon is the oldest annual marathon in the world and dates back to 1897. It is always held on Patriots' Day, the third Monday of April, and was inspired by the success of the first marathon competition at the 1896 Summer Olympics.

Race Result:

Pos.	Competitor	Country	Time	
1.	**Bill Rodgers**	**USA**	**2:09:27**	(Course record)
2.	Toshihiko Seko	Japan	2:10:12	
3.	Robert Hodge	USA	2:12:30	

TENNIS - U.S. OPEN

Tracy Austin and John McEnroe win their first Grand Slam titles at the 1979 U.S. Open.

Men's Singles Champion - John McEnroe - United States
Ladies Singles Champion - Tracy Austin - United States

The 1979 U.S. Open (formerly known as U.S. National Championships) was played on the outdoor hard courts at the USTA National Tennis Center in New York City. It was the 99th staging of the tournament and ran from August 28 to September 9.

Men's Singles Final

Country	Player	Set 1	Set 2	Set 3
United States	John McEnroe	7	6	6
United States	Vitas Gerulaitis	5	3	3

Women's Singles Final

Country	Player	Set 1	Set 2
United States	Tracy Austin	6	6
United States	Chris Evert	4	3

Men's Doubles Final

Country	Players	Set 1	Set 2
United States	John McEnroe / Peter Fleming	6	6
United States	Bob Lutz / Stan Smith	2	4

Women's Doubles Final

Country	Players	Set 1	Set 2
Netherlands / Australia	Betty Stöve / Wendy Turnbull	7	6
United States	Billie Jean King / Martina Navratilova	5	3

Mixed Doubles Final

Country	Players	Set 1	Set 2
South Africa	Greer Stevens / Bob Hewitt	6	7
Netherlands / South Africa	Betty Stöve / Frew McMillan	3	5

THE COST OF LIVING

America's favorite couple

Seven and Seven have been going together for over 40 years. For a perfect marriage, just pour 1½ oz. Seagram's 7 over ice in a tall glass, fill with 7-Up and enjoy our quality in moderation.

Seagram's 7 Crown
Where quality drinks begin.

COMPARISON CHART

	1979 Price	1979 Price Today	2018 Price	% Change
Annual Income	$7,200	$24,995	$57,817	+131.3%
House	$69,500	$241,276	$295,000	+22.3%
Car	$6,700	$23,260	$33,560	+44.3%
Gasoline (Gallon)	88¢	$3.06	$2.43	-20.6%
Milk (Gallon)	92¢	$3.19	$4.42	+38.6%
DC Comic Book	40¢	$1.39	$3.99	+187%

GROCERIES

Mrs Wrights White Bread (16oz)	29¢
Longhorn Style Cheddar Cheese (per lb)	$1.69
Puritan Peanut Butter (18oz)	89¢
CHB Strawberry Preserve (32oz jar)	99¢
Sather's Cookies (3x pkg.)	$1
Nature Valley Granola Bar (x2)	25¢
Blue Diamond Roasted Almonds (6oz can)	99¢
Leaf Whoppers Malted Milk Candy (8oz bag)	44¢
Chunky Chocolate Bar (2x 4oz)	88¢
Fritos Chee-Tos	59¢
Sweet Navel Oranges (3lb)	99¢
Red Delicious Apples (4lb)	99¢
Fresh Crisp Lettuce (large head)	33¢
U.S. No.1 Russett Potatoes (10lb bag)	79¢
Oberti Pitted Ripe Olives (#300 can)	53¢
Pacific Isle Mushrooms (4oz)	43¢
Round Rump Roast (per lb)	$1.79
New Zealand Leg Of Lamb (per lb)	$1.87
Fresh Butt Pork Steaks (per lb)	$1.69
Whole Grade A Fryers (per lb)	55¢
Jay's Couuntry Boy Bacon (1lb pkg.)	69¢
Fresh Pork Sausage (per lb)	98¢
Hereford Corned Beef (7oz can)	68¢
Hormel Chili With Beans (15oz can)	49¢
East Point Tiny Broken Shrimp (4½oz can)	93¢
Chicken Of The Sea Tuna (6½oz can)	67¢
Gorton's Clams (6½oz can)	69¢
Cup O'Noodles Instant Soup	39¢
Diet Delight Canned Fruit (16oz can)	49¢
Berstein Salad Dressing (8oz bottle)	59¢
Folgers Coffee (1lb)	$2.29
Coca-Cola (6 pack 12oz)	69¢
Tab-Coke (2 liter plastic bottle)	79¢
Sunkist Lemonade (12oz frozen)	29¢
Head & Shoulders Shampoo (15oz)	$2.42
Baby Shampoo (16oz bottle)	88¢
Neutrogena Soap (3½oz bar)	88¢
Mennon Speed Stick Deodorant	93¢
Listermint Mouthwash / Gargle (18oz)	$1.14
Colgate Toothpaste (9oz tube)	$1.49
Cascade Dishwasher Detergent (50oz box)	$1.44
Downy Fabric Softener (96oz)	$2.49
Pampers Disposable Diapers (box of 24)	$2.49
Vicks Cough Syrup (6oz)	$1.88
Chapstick Lip Balm	39¢
Bayer Asprin (x100)	99¢
100x Vitamin C Tablets (500mg)	$1.67
Soft N Pretty Toilet Tissue (4 roll pack)	89¢

EL RANCHO MARKET
27215 BASELINE • HIGHLAND

MONEY ORDERS 40¢ UP TO $200

BEST SERVICE IN TOWN

BLUE CHIP STAMPS

PRICES GOOD MARCH 15 THRU MARCH 21

LONGHORN **CHEESE** $1 69 LB.

LARGE MEATY PORK SPARERIBS........ 99¢ LB.

SLICED BEEF LIVER 69¢ LB.

BUTTERFISH FILLETS................ $1 09 LB.

BEEF TRIPE........ 49¢ LB.

TURKEY WINGS................ 49¢ LB.

FILLETS TURBOT FISH.... $1 39 LB.

COUPON
MEDIUM "AA" EGGS 49¢ DOZ.
LIMIT 2 DOZEN EXPIRES 3-21-79

COUPON
SPRINGFIELD SUGAR 5 LBS. 89¢
LIMIT 1 BAG EXPIRES 3-21-79

24-OZ. WESSON OIL 99¢

ANTHONY 1-LB. PKG. SPAGHETTI 45¢

SKIPPY 15-OZ.-6 CANS DOG FOOD $1 00

SCOTT SOFT 'N PRETTY 4 PK. TOILET TISSUE 89¢

SPECIAL VALUE 16-OZ. CAN CORN 3 FOR 89¢

SUAVE CLEAN HAIR 16-OZ. SHAMPOO 89¢

NESTLE SOUPTIME 4 ENV. 2.8 OZ. SOUP MIXES 49¢

SPECIAL VALUE 2-LB. GRAPE JELLY 99¢

SPECIAL VALUE 32-OZ. DISH DETERGENT 39¢

FRESH ICEBERG LETTUCE 3 HEADS $1

TASTY CALIFORNIA AVOCADOS 4 FOR $1

LONG GREEN CUKES 2 FOR 25¢

GREEN ONIONS or RADISHES 2 BUNCHES 25¢

U.S. NO. 1 PINTO BEANS 4 LBS $1

Frozen Foods *for quick warm weather meals*

JIMI'S 5-OZ. BURRITOS 4 FOR $1

SPECIAL VALUE VANILLA ICE CREAM ½ Gal. 99¢

SPECIAL VALUE 6-OZ. MEAT PIES 4 FOR $1

DAIRY and DELI FEATURES

PARKAY STICK - LB. MARGARINE 55¢

GOLDEN CREME ½ Gal. ORANGE JUICE $1 09

GOLDEN CREME 8-OZ. YOGURT 4 FOR $1

WEBERS BREAD 3 FOR 89¢ 16-OZ. loaf

CLOTHES

Women's Clothing

Aspen Poly Fill Parka	$70
Harris' Fall Dress	$16.99
Lightweight Italian V-Neck Sweater	$13.99
FedMart Fleece Sweater	$9.99
Rhonda Lee Peasant Blouse	$9.99
Long Sleeve Button Front Blouse	$3.99
Polyester Skirt	$8.99
Full Length Fleece Robe	$14.40
Bras (assorted styles)	$3.99
Panties / Bikinis (x3)	$7
Today's Girl Pany Hose	$1.09
Comfort-Top Knee-Hi Nylons (x4)	$1
JCPenny Mop Slippers	$5.99

Men's Clothing

Harris' Sports Coat	$49.99
Silverwoods Corduroy Vested Sport Suit	$79.90
Tux Shirt	$12.99
Velour Shirt	$6.44
Munsingwear Golf Shirt	$8.99
FedMart Fashion Print Shirt	$5
Hanes T-Shirts (x3)	$3.97
Harris' Better Slacks	$19.99
Britannia Casual Pants	$13.88
Wrangler Jeans	$10.50
Corduroy Flare-Leg Jeans	$8.97
Cotton Flannel Pajamas	$9.99
Mervyn's Jog Shorts	$6.99
Jockey Briefs	$2.19
Leather Belt	$2.99
JCPenny Slippers	$5.99

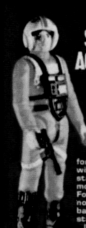
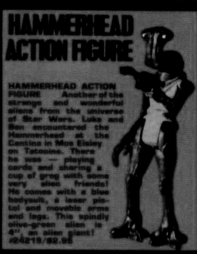
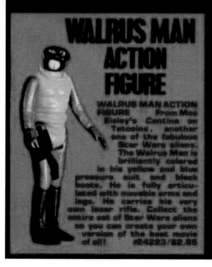

TOYS

Hedstrom 6½ft Topbar Play Center	$24.84
Empire Of Carolina Plastic Hot Cycle	$14.99
Cross River Umbroller Stroller	$12.93
Baby Little Love 14in Doll	$8.88
12½in Kiss Figure	$7.97
Boot Style Roller Skates	$29.99
Fisher Price Family Farm	$13.88
Tom Thumb Typewriter	$12.88
Darth Vader Tie Fighter	$8.88
Mattel Motor Putt Putt Railroad	$7.88
Mickey Mouse Turnover Choo-Choo	$8.88
Mego 6th Sense Game	$6.88
Mouse Trap Game	$6.66
Operation Game	$4.88
Hasbro Mickey Mouse Talking Phone	$10.99
Electronic Football Game	$14.99
H-G Pebbles & Bam Bam Sports Set	$1.69
Slinky Metal Spring Toy	99¢
Remco Bat Away Pitching Machine	$18.93
Mickey Rivers Fielders Glove	$9.96

ELECTRICAL GOODS

Quasar 25in Console Color TV	$499.88
RCA 19in XL-100 Color TV	$399.95
RCA 12in Sportable B&W TV	$104.99
RCA Video Cassette Recorder	$764
Zenith Integrated Stereo Sysytem	$259.95
Whirlpool 17.2 cu.ft Fridge / Freezer	$449
GE Potscrubber III Dishwasher	$299.95
Montgomery Ward 20lb Capacity Washer	$259.88
Maytag Dryer	$299.95
Litton Microwave	$277
GE FP2 Food Processor & Blender	$56.99
GE Toast-R-Oven	$36.99
Eureka Upright Vacuum Cleaner	$69.95
Safehouse Motion Detector Alarm	$199.95
Deluxe Cassette Phone Answering System	$299.95
Sanyo Portable Mini-Size AM Radio	$4.99

TOWN & COUNTRY PROPERTIES

COLD SPRING HARBOR
Water View

7 acres. 3 bedroom Cottage with Garages divisible. Extras include Barn, heated Pool, ideal Pavilion, attached Greenhouse. Tray ceiling Living Room, Panelled Den, Dining Room with views & fireplaces, super Kitchen & Solarium. 5 Bedrooms, 5 baths, ample servants. Luxurious, Low maintenance.

$500,000

FOXPOINT Ltd.
182 Birch Hill Rd.   Locust Valley, N.Y.
(516) 671-6110

OLD BROOKVILLE, LONG ISLAND

Every latest convenience is included in this handsome Williamsburg colonial newly constructed by one of Long Island's finest builders. Gracious and sunny rooms throughout with 9' ceilings, exquisite mouldings, pegged flooring, and fireplaces in large living room and in panelled family room. Lovely dining room and magnificent kitchen with walnut cabinetry, finest appliances, and ample eating area. Exceptionally large master bedroom with glamorous dressing room-bath plus four family bedrooms and servant's room with bath. All this on 2 wooded acres, well-landscaped and including a large brick terrace ideal for entertaining. $320,000.

JANE HAYES, INC.
92 Forest Avenue   Locust Valley, N.Y.
(516) 759-0400

OTHER ITEMS

Chevrolet Corvette	$12,313
Cadillac De Ville	$11,728
Oldsmobile Delta 88	$6,546
Pontiac Lemans	$5,888
Toyota Corolla	$3,698
Steel Belted LR78-15 Radial Tires	$63.70
Mileagemaker A78-13 Tires	$20.80
Sears 48 Battery (with trade-in)	$47.99
Happy Boy Car Wash & Wax	$2.79
Arror 10ft x 9ft Hamlet Shed	$109.99
Tappan 30in Gas Range	$398
JCPenny Countryside Sofa	$349
La-Z-Boy	$339
Weston 8ft Pool Table	$349.99
Nikon EM Camera	$259
Polaroid Onestep Camera	$28.87
LCD Quartz Chronograph Alarm Watch	$29.99
Ladies Timex Electric Watch	$33.99
14k Gold 3-Diamond Engagement Ring & Band	$245
Maxwell C90 CassetteTape (x3)	$2.85
Popov Vodka (1.75 liter)	$6.99
Cutty Sark Scotch (quart)	$9.79
Christian Bros. Brandy (quart)	$6.49
Blue Nun Liebfraumilch (magnum)	$6.99
Sebastiani Mountain Wine (1.5 liter)	$2.09

OG's are Old Gold Lights.
(and us who love 'em)

OG's are people who want a mellow smoke . . . a taste that is fulfilling, yet way down on tar. Old Gold Lights delivers. Smart cigarette OG — smart people OG's.

9 mg. tar

OLD GOLD LIGHTS

LOWERED TAR & NICOTINE

Warning: The Surgeon General Has Determined That Cigarette Smoking Is Dangerous to Your Health.

9 mg. "tar", 0.8 mg. nicotine av. per cigarette by FTC Method.

U.S. COINS

Official Circulated U.S. Coins		Years Produced
Half-Cent	½¢	1793 - 1857
Cent - Penny	1¢	1793 - Present
2-Cent (Bronze)	2¢	1864 - 1873
3-Cent (Nickle)	3¢	1865 - 1889
Trime (3-Cent Silver)	3¢	1851 - 1873
Half-Dime	5¢	1794 - 1873
Five Cent Nickel	5¢	1866 - Present
Dime	10¢	1796 - Present
20-Cent	20¢	1875 - 1878
Quarter	25¢	1796 - Present
Half Dollar	50¢	1794 - Present
Dollar Coin	$1	1794 - Present
Gold Dollar	$1	1849 - 1889
Quarter Eagle	$2.50	1796 - 1929
Three-Dollar Piece	$3	1854 - 1889
Four-Dollar Piece	$4	1879 - 1880
Half Eagle	$5	1795 - 1929
Gold Eagle	$10	1795 - 1933
Double Eagle	$20	1849 - 1933
Half Union	$50	1915

FORD MUSTANG '79

THE NEW BREED

Presenting a whole New Breed of Mustang for 1979. Dramatic new sports car styling gives this Mustang one of the most efficient aerodynamic designs of any car now built in America. With sports car features like a modified MacPherson front suspension, four-bar link rear suspension, rack and pinion steering and front stabilizer bar, all Mustangs have precise handling to help flatten corners.

The '79 Mustang offers a choice of engines (including the sporty 2.3 litre overhead cam as standard equipment), power trains and options to satisfy a wide range of driver needs. Available in 2-door or 3-door Hatchback models.

Experience the '79 Mustang for yourself with a test drive at your local Ford Dealer.

$4,458 As Shown
2-door sticker price.
Excluding title, taxes and destination charges.

FORD MUSTANG

FORD DIVISION *Ford*

58791007R00040

Made in the USA
Middletown, DE
08 August 2019